Designing
ePUBs
WITH
InDesign

Designing ePUBs with InDesign

David Bergsland

Radiqx
PRESS
MANKATO, MINNESOTA

Written and published in July, 2014
© David Bergsland • All Rights Reserved
ISBN-13: 978-1500692605
ISBN-10: 1500692603
Produced by Radiqx Press
314 Van Brunt Street
Mankato, Minnesota 56001
http://radiqx.com • info@radiqx.com

Please let me know if there is anyway I can help you in your publishing endeavors.

*This book is dedicated to fellow writers
and book designers trying
to keep a handle on
this rapidly changing endeavor.*

Contents

This book covers the update to InDesign CC 2014

An edited version of Adobe's official list for the new InDesign 10:

One of the largest efforts was put into ePUB export: Not only do we get fixed layout ePUB3s, but there have been many improvements to tables [stroke, fill, and more] plus drag-n-drop columns & rows—especially in fixed layout where they can output virtually anything InDesign can produce.

- **Fixed Layout (FXL) and Reflowable EPUB Export**
  - Live text that is selectable and searchable in FXL
  - Ability to include audio, video and Edge Animate content in FXL
  - Several other improvements in EPUB export, including writing stroke and fill, control over CSS width and height, improved support for tables, preview apps etc.
  - Enhanced Metadata Controls in Export Dialogs
  - Expanded Export dialogs for FXL and Reflowable ePUBs
  - Additional accessibility support in EPUB through epub:type attribute

- **Drag and Drop Table Columns and Rows**

- **Enhanced Package with IDML and PDF**

- **Seamless Update:** the automatic and manual migration of local settings from previous release to current release

- **Find Previous**

CHAPTER ONE

Beginning your ePUB design

Here I am again recommending a road less traveled by—not unusual in my life and work. Before the choruses rise up in defense of other workflows, let me tell you my reasonings. I fully recognize that most people write in Word and many produce their ebooks in Word. Many more code their ebooks by hand in HTML, CSS, and Javascript. What these people do not realize [in most cases] is this simple fact starts their book under a great handicap. Many of the very effective typographic tools for communication are simply missing, If they are publishing their own book, Word simply does not provide many of the best tools for communicating clearly and easily with their readers.

I begin with a fully formatted book— the print version or the ePUB FXL

These versions allow me to develop the typography of the book and have the most tools to communicate clearly and comfortably with the reader. The key is that all portions of the book: paragraphs, tables, and graphics must be formatted with styles. Only this will give you the global control of the book you need to make effective conversions for the various distributors like Lightning source, Createspace, Lulu, Kindle KDP, the iBooks Store, NookPress, Kobo Writing Life, Smashwords, Draft2Digital, Scribd, Gumroad, and so on. The entire process is covered in *Writing In InDesign CC 2014 Pro-*

ducing Books. This book is concerned with the conversion to the various ebook formats: downloadable color PDFs, ePUBs—both fixed layout and reflowable, with and without embedded fonts, and the adjustments necessary to make your ePUBs convert well to Kindle books.

Books are not entirely about words

Of course as a writer this may not make much sense to you. But please hear me out. For years I have taught graphic designers that the content is all that matters. Now I am teaching writers that presentation and layout are a big part of your book. For designers, this has been a major fight because many never read the copy they design into books and printed materials. Now I am dealing with writers who do not see the need for typography and layout skills.

Most designers do not deal well with words

Graphic designers [and this includes most book designers] are visual people, focused on how things look. One of my major concerns as I started to write books in the mid-1990s was my experience in my digital publishing classes using published textbooks only as bad examples providing poor communication. As a pastor, commercially available Bible studies were just as bad. They were normally almost impossible to read or use—being more focused on style than communication. The examples are endless.

My pursuit of functional, reader-centered books has been fraught with trials. I was constantly bumping up against standardized procedures of traditional publishers which really made their books hard to read or use effectively. This focus on the reader is so far outside the norm in publishing today that there is no room at all for an author who even cares about these things (except in this brand new world of on-demand self-publishing).

Let's talk about some simple examples of this lack of concern for the reader

Illustrations listed by number with no connection to the copy which talks about what is illustrated: Most traditional non-fiction publishers require this typographic horror. In many cases, authors are not allowed to even pick out the images because they are not considered professional enough to understand what is required of an graphic.

The results are illustrations, maps, charts, and photos listed by number which are often not on the same page (or even the same chapter) as the content they illustrate. *Why bother to even have them?* Few readers will find them or take the time to look for them. The result is frustrated readership and readers who simply quit reading in disgust.

For fiction, it is equally bad to have an illustration or map which cannot be easily referenced by the reader. In my novels I add maps where they are needed in the copy to help the reader understand what is going on. Remember, the goal is to assist the reader. For ebooks, I am giving each important map a chapter heads in the Table of Contents.

Heads and subheads generated by designers: In many cases over the years I spent as a graphic designer, I wrote all the subheads, developed all the lists, wrote all the captions, and even wrote most of the headlines.

I developed them out of a need to help direct the reader through the copy I was formatting. The author commonly had no clue that they were desirable or necessary. I formatted them as a service to the reader. But I was a real minority as mentioned. Many designers do not even read the copy they lay out, as I said.

As a writer, you must be aware of these issues and realize that they are a primary method of clearing up communication with the reader. Heads, subheads, list design, and all the rest are key elements of your support of easy understanding by the reader.

Page layout determined by fashion and visual concerns: In the graphic design world, fonts are often chosen because they look good. Layouts are determined by fashion. Columns, margins, sidebars and the like are chosen to stimulate visual interest and provoke excitement instead of being chosen to communicate the content effectively, clearly, and accessibly. Clarity and accuracy are rarely considered.

The most glaring example of this is seen in the books where content is broken up into small pieces—supposedly to help people with short attention spans. We recently bought a creationism book that is virtually unreadable. The gorgeous, fancy illustrations push the copy into bits and pieces that are lost in the visual clutter of the pages' backgrounds. My wife gave up on it and asked me for a verbal report.

But it goes much further than that. Here's a quote from Wikipedia about the normal traditional editorial process (I realize it is difficult to read):

> "*(Once)* a decision is taken to publish a work, and the technical legal issues resolved, the author may be asked to improve the quality of the work through rewriting or smaller changes, and the staff will edit the work. Publishers may maintain a house style, and staff will copy edit to ensure that the work matches the style and grammatical requirements of each market. Editors often choose or refine titles and headlines. Editing may also involve structural changes and requests for more information. Some publishers employ fact checkers, particularly regarding non-fiction works."

Notice that there is nothing here about serving the readers. The readers' needs are not part of the process. It's all about sales and the marketing decisions of the publisher. This is equally true for secular and spiritual publishers. Textbooks are some of the worst examples of editorial damage. The reader's needs seldom take priority.

In most cases they will not even talk to you as an author unless you can convince them that you have a large enough following to guarantee enough sales to cover the costs. Once you've passed that hurdle, they will normally insist that you fit your content into their style—even if that style hinders your book and may even offend your readers.

You must learn to produce your own books.

For the past two decades, I have taught digital publishing skills. During that time I have written and published books, both traditionally and on-demand. I have taught skills to present digital content transparently, effectively, and gracefully. But Word [and word processors in general] cannot do this. There are skills and capabilities that are necessary which are simply not available in Office. It is true, that ePUBs and Kindle books cannot do many of these things either. But unless you know about these things and have developed the skill to produce them, your ePUBs will not be pleasant experiences for your readers.

Quality levels required for professional publishing

- **Typography:** The skill to use fonts, paragraph styling, and page layout to invisibly communicate content: point size, leading, small caps, ligatures, oldstyle figures, lining figures, ems, ens, discretionary hyphens, tracking, kerning, and much more. All of these things are controlled with styles: paragraph, character, and object. For this you need a professional page layout program. Many of these things are not yet available in ePUBs unless you use specialized fonts.

- **High resolution, full-color images:** You want vector graphics if possible. Printing requires 300 dpi minimum for photos and bitmapped images. You'll need Photoshop for the high resolution images. They need to be PDFs, EPSs, AIs, PSDs, or TIFFs for printing quality work. For ePUBs you'll be using color and the highest resolutions possible on a practical level. JPEGs, GIFs, and PNGs are necessary, but FXL images work better at 150 dpi.

  Covers must be created at high resolution to enable all the various sizes required by Apple, Amazon, B&N, and so on. Kindle is currently requesting that "For best quality, your image would be 2820 pixels on the shortest side and 4500 pixels on the longest side" for the JPEGs uploaded for your Kindle books. That is a very large image: 9.4" x 15" at 300 dpi—plus it is not in the normal 600x800 size ratio which has been recommended for ePUB images.

- **Page layout:** A thorough understanding of columns, margins, alignments, indents, gutters, lists, tables, headlines, subheads, sidebars, running heads, drop caps, and much more is required. Just a simple sidebar with a text wrap around the overlapping portions of copy is much more complex in a reflowable ePUB even though it is a simple thing in an ePUB FXL or downloadable PDF..

I'll do my best to remember to define all these terms as I go. Some of you already know quite a bit of this—if you've been using InDesign before. But, to produce a professional book of excellent quality these things must be taken into account.

Writing and editing in InDesign gives you layout power

Until you've tried it, you will find it hard to imagine the power of writing and editing fully formatted. You can see the page as it develops and adjust things to help the reader understand your points. You really can help the reader comprehend your message. That's what excellent book design is all about.

You can use a subhead for clarity, a kicker as a small lead-in style to emphasize a header, lists to recapture the reader's attention with their rhythmic order, a sidebar for peripheral information to entertain the good readers, a table for overly complex lists, and much more.

Even more important, you can add graphics and illustration in the midst of the content which talks about that artwork. Charts, graphics, closeups, diagrams, and info-graphics can be an immense help to your readers. This is where page layout apps like InDesign truly shine. Photoshop is part of the package. Plus, InDesign can produce graphics faster and often better than specialized illustration apps like Illustrator.

You will be able see on the page, as you write, how clearly the content is being communicated—or not. It helps you change your content into something that communicates clearly and easily to your readers. It lets you see boring areas and fix them as you write. It provides the control you need to speak to your specific niche—emphasizing unique niche concepts as you go. You can also see when you've gone too far and lapsed into mere busyness and clutter.

Basically writing in a page layout program gives you tools that word processors have a hard time even imagining— which could not be accomplished in that glorified typewriter even if you perceived the need. You will learn to communicate much more clearly. You'll focus on the readers more easily and on what you can do to help them. You can actually try to put yourself in the readers' shoes and answer their questions using both the content and the layout.

CHAPTER TWO

Reality orientation

But let's face it, beginning authors don't normally have the foresight to do something like this—in most cases. By the time you are considering doing something like what we are discussing, you have commonly published a book or more. If you are just starting out, the good news is that books like this will show you what you need to do to produce excellent books. It takes time to learn how to write, how to communicate clearly, how to convert the vision you've been given, plus the actual nuts and bolts required to work in reality. This is grown-up work (no matter what your actual physical age is).

Plus, there is a lot to learn: typography, page layout, printing limitations, ebook limitations, and much more. BUT! You can do it simply, line upon line, precept upon precept, as you grow into the publisher you need to be.

How long will it take?

That depends on how seriously you take the work of book production. I used to teach this in two intense semesters to people starting from scratch who were not interested in writing. Most just wanted to draw. As a writer this will come more easily.

You can be up and running in a week or so, competent in a matter of months, and producing excellent work within a year.

But you will need to work at it and practice. In this new publishing paradigm, we can publish blog postings, white papers, books, booklets, essays, teachings, Bible studies, prophecies, forecasts, guides, novels, press releases, media kits, and more. Of course, this assumes that you are writing on your computer. That is required. If so, you already have a computer and some software. The question is whether or not it can do what you need it to do. Some upgrades may be necessary, though you'll be surprised at how little is actually required.

Let's start with the computer. The main thing is that ebooks are so new that current software is required. This requires a relatively new computer. What I am listing as minimums are based on the assumption that you will be using the Adobe Creative Suite or Creative Cloud in a recent version. At the least, you'll need InDesign CC 2014. This is especially true for ebooks for fixed layout ePUB export just began there. For Photoshop, CS4 or better will work.

Computer minimums

* **You really need a Mac:** but I won't argue about it. You'll need a 64-bit Intel CPU or better, a monitor at least 1600 pixels wide [2000 pixels or more is better], 8 GB or more of RAM [but you really need 16 GB], Mac OSX.7 or better [Windows 7 or better], a 300 GB hard drive or better, and safe backup storage. You'll need a full extended keyboard with a numerical keypad and the editing keys. If you have a laptop with all its limitations, you'll want a wired USB or Bluetooth keyboard with a full set of function keys, editing keys, and a numerical keypad.

The numerical keypad is essential for style shortcuts and the editing keys are necessary for easy navigation through your book. You will really slow your production speed and you'll not like InDesign without the full keyboard. It's needed for custom shortcuts, and many of the standard ones like page navigation.

If you already have a PC: you can use it providing it meets the criteria above. Plus you'll need to be able to calibrate your monitor.

These are all minimums. You'll actually want the 16 GB RAM to keep working at speed and to avoid crashes. Each book will add at least a large portion of a Gigabyte into storage. So a 500–1000 GB hard drive is not out of line at all.

🐾 **You'll also need high-speed internet and a PostScript printer for proofing:** You will be uploading and downloading PDFs that are often dozens of megabytes in size, commonly many times in a day. It often cannot be done at all with a slow internet connection. You will also be doing all your marketing online and you do not want to be wasting time with slow access.

InDesign requires a PostScript printer for accurate proofs. However, your printed proofs can done elsewhere. Also, the best proof is a single printed book from your on-demand printing company (like Lightning source, Createspace, or Lulu).

For ePUB proofs I recommend an iPad as the best quality and most versatile, but for Kindle proofs a high-definition Fire really helps.

InDesign CC2014, but CS5 is fine for the rest ◇◇◇◇◇◇◇◇

You'll want InDesign CC, at least, at $20 a month. But the full CC package is only $50 a month. Actually, you can get by with CS4 or even CS3 for Illustrator, Photoshop, and the rest, but you need InDesign CC 2014. Every version does substantially better ePUBs and fixed layout ePUBs require CC 2014 or better.

Get the non-profit or academic versions: (if you qualify). A good resource for these discounts and information on whether you qualify or not is found at the AcademicSuperstore Website. They just need a valid school ID or a scan of your non-profit paperwork, certificate, or whatever. Yes, it is worth taking an accredited class to access academic pricing. Remember, learning to produce your own books will save you $500 to $2000 for every book published. Publishing even two books a year will cover your software expenses.

Except for InDesign, you can buy old versions from eBay and other similar venues: You will need InDesign, Photoshop, and

Acrobat Pro: You may need Dreamweaver. Illustrator is handy. But as I mentioned, older versions of these applications will do fine for you—except for InDesign.

In this field you must keep up

Because of all the changes coming with HTML5, CSS3, and ePUB3 you'll need to keep current software. Plus, make sure you have a computer which can handle the new versions. I had to buy a new computer to work with CS5 back in 2009. You need to plan on a new PC computer every couple of years. Macs last quite a bit longer. My old computer still runs fine. My wife is using it. But I can no longer use it for my work. I was forced to get a new computer this winter with 16 GB RAM primarily because of Mavericks and I am beginning to work with video. But notice that I got five years out of the old one and it still works fine for everything but book production. It's hard to beat the iMac. It's designed for people like us.

CHAPTER THREE

Page layout basics

Setting up your book to be read: One of the more daunting aspects of book design for the inexperienced is page layout. Most people have Word experience and as I have said countless times already—Word cannot do professional page layout. In fact, it is worse than that because Word's attempts give you bad habits and poor expectations—which must be corrected. This takes both time and money.

Many settings have to be covered for every document. Many of these are set up as you go through the Preferences in InDesign. Every application has important decisions to be made in Preferences. To repeat, the point is to set up your applications so they work best for you. But all I can really do for Word users is tell you to keep it simple and consistent using styles so that the conversion to InDesign is faster and easier. Yes, ePUBs require fully formatted content.

Before I get started with this, I need remind you of the goal: a beautiful book which is comfortable to read. You need a customized set of styles to enable you to keep your book consistent and give you global control over the entire book as you format. Excellent typography is only possible if you understand how to design paragraphs. Styles make paragraph design possible. We will deal with them conceptually, but you should know this is why InDesign is so good. These options often step outside the entire paradigm of a word processor.

Designing your paragraphs

I need to share a little about setting up your paragraphs. Most of this knowledge is assumed by software manuals and publishing Websites. Somehow they seem to believe that your little psyche will be stifled if any opinion on normalcy is mentioned—or some such idiocy like that. It's not magic or luck when you produce reading materials that are enjoyable to read. It is the result of setting your copy up (formatting it) in a manner that the reader instantly recognizes and comfortably understands.

In this book, focused on ebooks and particularly ePUBs, I have to assume you know the basics about designing and using paragraph, character, table, and object styles. If you do not, you need the full versions: *Writing In InDesign Producing Books* for the software version you are using.

You must lead the reader through your writing effortlessly—completely unaware of your guidance. You need to make your writing feel natural, comfortable, and obvious to help the reader receive the content.

 **My way is not the only way:** As I go through this little presentation, I will be simply sharing what I use. My hope is that you can look at my usage for conceptual understanding. Then convert that for your use. I will attempt to give you the arguments that have convinced me to do things in this manner. But, there is no right or wrong (once you are inside the relatively wide parameters of normalcy).

Our basic problem is that we have too much to read. Subconsciously virtually everyone looks for ways to eliminate content (in order to keep reading requirements within a tolerable range). We might miss a lot of good content this way—but that is the way it is.

In our modern culture, huge numbers of people have difficulty reading. People often know how to read (technically) but they hate to actually do it. I've heard stats as high as 60% of Americans are functionally illiterate. Most people agree it is a huge percentage even if it is as low as a third of adults. They may be able to read [literate in the polls], but it is difficult for them, in a second language, or they just hate reading [so in practice they rarely or never read]. A Pew Research poll that came out in early April of 2012 says that nearly a quarter of Americans did not read a single book the previous year. The social media users go far beyond that, of course. I know many young men and women (fifty years old or less) who avoid reading entirely [or as much as possible]—even though they are considered fully literate by polls and testing. Many have college degrees.

The need for comfort

The result is that we must go out of our way to make our books accessible to poor readers. Reading is hard to avoid. But many do. We have a large and growing portion of our middle class who get all of their information from social media, TV, movies, and videos.

 **Modern interactive features:** This is an area you need to thoroughly examine. My opinion is that adding video and such to a book changes it into something entirely different. The non-reader may be more attracted to the video content, BUT would they ever buy a "book" in the first place? If you feel the need for video, you should consider whether you actually need a "book" at all.

We can argue all we want about these media options and their limited amount of actual content. But, this fact remains: even those who buy our books may well have trouble reading. We must help them as much as we can with our formatting and layout. We must be kind to our readers—gentle and loving. If our readers experience any discomfort or reading difficulty we have probably lost them. They will simply not finish reading our content. This must become your basic, bottom line focus for your book designs.

I am a very good and very fast reader. Yet I simply put books aside that are difficult to read—unless the content is required or very compelling. I am not talking about difficult content (though that can be a problem). I am talking about poor layouts, columns that are too wide, fonts that are too stylized, overly busy layouts, and all the rest.

A couple of years ago I was struggling with a book on creationism (I've mentioned already that my wife gave up and asked me to brief her on it when I finished reading it). The content is exciting. The layout is so poor with photographic backgrounds, glossy paper, excessive line lengths and a host of other problems—I had to force myself to read it. The only difference with me is that I am tuned into this problem so I often notice when I do this with a book. Most people are not conscious of why they put down a book. They simply do not read it.

The poetry filter

Here's another example. I wonder how many of you are like me? I probably shouldn't admit this, but anything in a book which is formatted as poetry I skip (except in scripture). I simply pass over that portion of the copy and continue on. My experience over the years is that the content in poetry is very limited and far too open to interpretation. I am almost always looking for facts—easily accessible facts. In a novel, I am looking for plot and character development. Poetry has never provided this for me. So, I have developed reading habits that keep me from wasting time. I jump to the explanation of the poetry that inevitably follows.

I am sure this horrifies many of you. I am not saying that this poetry filter of mine is good or desirable. I am simply saying that it exists. Again, the only thing strange is that [as a typographer] I am more aware of my reading habits—so I noticed this behavior.

What reading filters do you have? More importantly, what reading filters do your readers have? You need to know: I suspect you need to examine yourself. It's hard to say what you have been missing all these years. We all have things we just do not read—often for subconscious reasons. As typographers we try to limit those reactions. At the very least, we need to be aware of possible issues.

For example, in one of the author groups of which I am a member, we had an extended argument about the amount of description needed in a novel. It appeared that in general the younger the reader the less important they considered description to be. The older the reader, in general, the more they thought excellent descriptions kept books from feeling thin, less weighty, or underdeveloped.

The best way to find out what's available is in styles

In InDesign, virtually anything that is possible to do to a paragraph is available. So, to talk about the typography of paragraphs we need to go through the options available in paragraph and character styles. This will show you some or many things you had no idea were even possibilities.

In this book, I am skipping this with the assumption that you already know these materials. If you do not, you need to learn what is necessary; what is possible; what works, and, most importantly, what improves readability. In *Writing In InDesign* I have 160 pages covering this basic knowledge to get you up and running.

CHAPTER FOUR

Book production

Let's start with a brief review of the process to make sure we are on the same page: Again, this is a very complex process. It is not particularly difficult, but the procedure is certainly not simple. This is subject to fashion, but be careful.

The book production process

Get the vision: You start with your idea. You research the market and try to determine your niche. This is an area fraught with uncertainty, because you really have no idea if it will sell or who will buy it. Even free books need to be positioned to attract readers looking for your specific content.

Pick a size: This again is more complicated than it looks and largely applies to print. But in another way it is no real problem. Anything you choose to start with can easily be reformatted to another size once everything is in place and completely controlled by styles. When in doubt start with a 6×9 page for print. For your ePUBs, I recommend a 6" x8" page for fixed layout and a 600x800 pixel text frame for reflowable.

You need to pray about this or at least seriously think about it. Many times I have been led to a specific size to use for a particular book. Remember who is going to use your book. Know the demographics of your future (and commonly unknown to you as yet) group of readers—your niche. Often it will surprise you once you actually begin selling your book.

For InDesign, you need to plan things out a bit: You will eventually have many different formats and page sizes. I am just using a Primary Text Frame and doing my additional formats individually. I find I usually need to write new copy or produce new graphics—especially for the ePUBs and Kindle versions where special fonts don't work well and the graphics need to be so radically converted. I used to always start with print and write for all formats. More recently (as I am doing for this book), I am starting with the fixed layout ePUB and building the other versions off of it.

❧ **Using your set of default styles begin writing or adding pieces:** All you do is type Command+Num6 (or what ever shortcut you use for your headline style) and start writing. If you are using pieces from essays, blog posts, booklets or whatever else you have written to be a part of this, just paste them in order and format as you go.

❧ **If you are using Word:** Place the Word doc into InDesign and reformat it into your styles. The styles from Word are missing too much to use effectively.

❧ **You need to keep these styles fluid in your mind:** One of the real blessings of using styles is that you can develop your book style over the first few chapters. There will be a real ebb and flow as you adjust your styles—especially your paragraph spacing— as you watch the pages come together.

Front matter & back matter

You need to add your front and back matter as you are putting the book together. You need to be thinking about the entire package throughout the writing and production of the book. There are several (often many) pages of materials that need to be at the front and back of your book. Many of them are optional. Several are not. Some are required for print but not used for ebooks. For example, in print, you must have a title page and a copyright page. You almost certainly need a Table of Contents (the actual type should not be in an ebook though the setup must be done). You may or may not need an introduction, a dedication, or any of about a dozen other possibilities. You should have an index for non-fiction The following is deeply indebted to Wikipedia and the volunteer writers and editors who have spent so much time putting information like this together.

Front matter choices

- **Advertising blurbs and testimonials:** This would include lists of additional books by the author and quotes from reviewers. I know they are commonplace, but they are certainly gauche.

    Though this is merely my opinion, such self-aggrandizing always seems a bit desperate and is bragging at best (be it on your head).

- **Half Title:** This page just has the title—no subtitle, author name, or anything else. It is the first page inside the cover. You normally use the title font and style from the cover, but smaller. Not used in ePUBs.

- **Frontispiece:** This is an illustration on the page facing the title page. An old German title page with frontispiece from 1722 [WIKIMEDIA COMMONS]. As you can see to the right, this can be a very stylish and elegant way to start your book. If done well, it offers comfort and tradition to your book design. You should consider this. But it's difficult to use in Reflowable ePUBs.

- **Title page:** In print, this page is commonly a reduced version of your book cover in grayscale, unless you use a frontispiece. Ideally the title page shows the title of the work, the person or group responsible for its intellectual content, the place & year of publication, and the name of the publisher. For ePUBs you use the cover.

- **Copyright page:** This is normally on the back of the title page. Some would say that it is absolutely required to be there. It contains copyright owner name and the year, the publishing staff, edition and printing information, ISBN, cataloging details for the Library Of Congress. The lawyers love this page in a big publishing house. Hopefully, we are more merciful than that.

- **Table of contents:** This is built and updated with the Table of Contents... command at the bottom of the Layout menu. It's powerful and I have a tendency to add too much. I am in the process of rethinking my TOC use. I'm moving smaller subhead content to the index. But it works well in print, downloadable PDF, and ePUBs. In the ebooks, the entries even have live links to the indicated copy.

- **List of figures:** This is more needed for fine art books than anything, but this would be the place it goes. It is also produced with the TOC commands. You'll need special paragraph styles for your captions which can then be collected.

- **List of tables:** If your book is data-driven, this might be a good service for your readers. This is also produced with the TOC commands. You'll need special paragraph styles for your table headers which can then be collected.

- **Dedication:** This where you name the people whose inspiration enabled you to write the book. In ePUBs, it's usually at the end of the book.

- **Acknowledgments:** These are all the people, groups, and Websites who helped you. In ePUBs, it's usually at the end of the book.

- **Foreword:** This is written by a real person, other than yourself.

- **Preface:** This covers the story of how the book came into being, or how the idea for the book was developed. It often includes the acknowledgments.

❧ **Introduction:** Here you can give the purpose, goals, and organization of your book. This is where you tell the reader the devices you use throughout the book [like little graphics for tips, how you will identify sources, and things like that].

❧ **Prologue:** Written by the narrator or a character in the book, this gives the setting and background details, some earlier story that ties into this book, or other relevant details. It sets the stage for the real content.

Many of these things are not necessary or even desirable for all books. You need to be careful that you don't bore the reader into tears—to the place where they simply put the book down because it is too much trouble to get to the actual content of the book. [Which is why they bought the book in the first place, remember?]

Back matter choices

There are many options here also. These are more reader services and references to help them as they read your book. Where much of the front matter helps fiction, the back matter is almost entirely for non-fiction. Of course, Tolkien loved to add back matter about Middle Earth—which further developed the reality of his fictional world.

 **It's all up to you . However , if you ignore all of these things , the reader might well feel the book is not complete .**

❧ **Epilogue:** This is a great service to the reader in fiction. For me and my wife anyway, we often talk about books that just dump you off with many of the issues unresolved. We want completion, a sense that we know what happened and that it's all OK.

To quote from Wikipedia:

"An epilogue is a final chapter at the end of a story that often serves to reveal the fates of the characters. Some epilogues may feature scenes only tangentially related to the subject of the story. They can be used to hint at a sequel or wrap up all the loose ends. They can occur at a significant period of time after the main plot has ended. In some cases, the epilogue has been used to allow the main character a chance to 'speak freely'. An epilogue can continue in the same narrative style and perspective as the preceding story, although the form of an epilogue can occasionally be drastically different from the overall story."

- **Afterword:** "When the author steps in and speaks directly to the reader, that is more properly considered an afterword."

- **Conclusion:** This is also called a summary or a synopsis.

- **Appendix/Addendum:** This contains additional materials to flesh out a particular portion of the book. You should consider this option as a reader service. As Appendices they can work really well. But, they can also be released as separate booklets for readers of earlier editions and for more advanced readers who might otherwise skip your book.

- **Glossary:** Relevant word definitions

- **Bibliography:** Books used and additional readings

- **Index:** Word and phrase references by page

- **Errata:** No longer needed for on-demand publishing. We simply upload a revised version.

- **Colophon:** "With the development of the private press movement from around 1890, colophons became conventional in private press books, and often included a good deal of additional information on the book, including statements of limitation, data on paper, ink, type and binding, and other technical details. Some such books include a separate 'Note about the type', which will identify the names of the primary typefaces used, provide a brief description of the type's history and a brief statement about its most identifiable physical characteristics." [Wikipedia]

  This is just a fun addition, especially for a book like this that is about book production. Come to think of it: I have forgotten to do this. Let me go do that now———***Done!***

Hopefully, you've been thinking about these things

The appropriate time to add front matter and back matter is during the writing of the book. A passage may suggest an appendix. For example, as I was editing in the Writing In InDesign book, I noticed that it was really confusing to refer the reader to my Website to get the instructions to add the basic paragraph styles with which to start your use of them. It seemed good to add the step-by-step for a basic set of styles to this book.

Concern for reader confusion may lead to a prologue to ease them into the main story or content. Mainly you need to be aware that all of these other things exist. Then you will develop them in process while you are writing. It's not good to start dealing with them after everything is written. Often you've forgotten the incidents that will trigger good reader service content like this.

Again! It's all about the reader

Continuously, you must consider how to serve the reader. You are writing for them. They deserve all the help you can give them. Often you must radically shift things.

For example, in my verse by verse Bible studies it finally dawned on me that I was raising an almost impenetrable barrier to reading the book. I had an introduction/prologue that included doctrinal statements, a short testimony (it grew with each book), and more. The short testimony of my spiritual walk at the front of the book finally grew to over a half dozen pages and was keeping the readers from reaching the real content. So, I changed it to a reference in the introduction and moved it to an afterword in the back matter.

In fact, for a while I moved much of this material to the back of all my books in multiple appendices. I leave a brief listing of the appendixes available and then go on with the main part of the book. I did this to give the reader easier access to the real content. Try to watch yourself as you read other books to see what you find irritating.

Excessive front matter

This is especially true of ebooks. This is where I first actually noticed the problem. Front matter is really jarring there. There is really no comfortable way to flip pages and skip to the actual content in an ebook. So you want to get the reader there quickly. I have eliminated or moved all the front matter in all my ebooks except for a very brief copyright statement and the dedication.

But there is no right or wrong here. You need to determine what your reader would like. You might ask them in your blog. For sure, ask your reviewers. Make sure you have people from your target audience doing your reviews. Above all do not use these devices to "bulk up"your book. That's a subtle form of fraud. If the content is not necessary, do not add it to your book.

The need for features of the book will become apparent as you are writing. In this brief book I'm avoiding more of the background and simply trying to set you up so you have the knowledge you need to get started with ePUBs.

CHAPTER FIVE

The various ebook formats

All of InDesign's output is an ebook

As you know, almost all of InDesign's output is in ebook form. Even for the print book, we produce a PDF. This PDF reads wonderfully well in iBooks or any ereader which can handle PDFs. However, even that PDF should really be modified for excellent use as a downloadable PDF. The graphics can all be in color, for example.

Now that ePUBs and Kindle books have reached the tipping point [become more than 50% of sales for most of us], we truly need to be sure we make a excellent ebook for sale. At this point, my best sales are still through Createspace [Amazon's print service]. Kindle KDP remains second but all of this is changing fairly quickly. Everything other than Amazon is now my largest portion of sales. Both the iBooks Store and Kobo are now growing faster than Kindle. Nook is shooting itself in the foot.

I've almost completely quit using the KDP Select option which allows me to offer the book for free by giving Amazon exclusivity for three months or more. The free option doesn't seem to work well for anyone other than writers of romances or more distasteful genre like erotica, horror, and so on.

Basically we need to learn to be fluid on these things. There are new startups [almost weekly] trying to break the monopoly Amazon now stakes out on a pure ease of shopping and book discovery level. As soon as one of them gains traction [Tomely, Draft2Digital, and at least a dozen more today], book selling will go to the next level. We desperately need an excellent shopping service for ebooks for Christians, for example. CBD [Christian Book Distributors] is the best on prices, but the shopping experience is not good. They use a proprietary ereader that is very restrictive. Overall, outside of Amazon, the ebook shopping experiences are still at a very rudimentary level.

InDesign is getting much better

There is still a long ways to go, but there is a good deal of hope that future versions of InDesign CC will give us what we need to produce excellent ebooks without any need to do hand-coding. InDesign CS6 was a good step better than InDesign CS5.5. InDesign CC 2014 is really getting pretty close now. Almost all of our problems now are with the distributors and ereaders.

Now that Windows is the second-largest OS and will soon be the third largest—after Android and iOS—there may well be further changes. At this point, it does not appear likely that a tablet [iOS or Android] could handle an app like InDesign. But as the desktop computer fades into niche work, as MacOS blends into iOS, we do not know what the future will bring.

This book is current to the release of CC 2014. But this is a rapidly changing industry. As usual, new information will be posted on *The Skilled Workman* until there is enough to do the next edition of this book.

ePUB & Kindle design in InDesign

I need to mention two basic assumptions.

- **First of all, you need the book completely written, edited, and proof read:** It's very painful to format a book that is not completed, unless you are actually writing in InDesign [which I recommend, as you know]. Plus, you certainly do not want a situation where you make changes in the ePUB which need to be added to the print version and on and on.

- **Secondly, you need to have the book completely formatted for print or fixed layout in InDesign:** This means that all copy is formatted with styles: paragraph, character, table, cell, and object styles. No local formatting is acceptable. If it is not completely formatted, you will have no way to control your ePUB globally and you will waste many hours and probably many days, weeks, or months.

Once you have your book finished & formatted for print or FXL

You are ready to start. Why do we start with fixed layouts? Simply put: many of the quality extras you can use to help communicate with your readers are not available in reflowable ePUBs and Kindle books [HTML/CSS]. Fixed layout ePUBs or neither fish nor fowl. InDesign has done some very complex coding to get around the HTML/CSS limitations of an ePUB.

This is especially true of your graphics. Though you can add color in any area you like, the resolution of your graphics will be very poor — 72 dpi in HTML compared to 2400 dpi for vector graphics or 300 dpi for continuous tone [Photoshop] in print. FXL ePUBs work better with 150 dpi. From print or FXL you can start the process of dumbing things down to fit within the limitations of HTML, CSS, and ePUB2. If you make a mistake or change your mind about anything, you need the high resolution, typographically excellent master from which you can start again.

Once you have that baseline, the modifications necessary for your ebooks become relatively easy—though never simple. At this point, for example, you need three versions for the font variations alone. Plus, for books like this one, you'll need the new option of ePUB Fixed Layout [FXL]. This is a real good option for the iBooks Store and Kobo. For reflowable ebooks, iBooks & KF8 [Kindle Fire], enable you to embed any font you have a license to use. For Nook, Kobo, e-ink Kindles, and all the various tablet apps you need to keep it simple with 4-font serif and sans serif font families. The e-ink ebooks can't handle font info at all. We'll talk about other changes as we go through. Some are very important.

Designing & formatting your ePUB & Kindle book without coding

With my assumption [that you have a finished, formatted and uploaded book] comes another equally important expectation. Writers and designers don't normally do well with code. It's not that we cannot understand it or use it. It's more like it is so boring and stifling to creativity that we simply avoid it whenever possible. My experience is that people like us can handle a little simple Web coding like XHTML and CSS (actually, most of us have been forced into it for our Websites). However, most people who do what we do really dislike coding. It is a specialized skill not found often in creative people. Even HTML and CSS code writing is a painful process.

The question is how do we take these givens and produce an ePUB and a Kindle version of excellent quality? It is not difficult, but you are certainly going to need to rethink your definition of book and of typographic excellence.

Do fancy ePUBs still require fancy coding?

Prior to CC 2014, ePUB design was commonly produced by coding specialists. This practice will continue for large publishers who can afford a dedicated ebook department. But, it's no longer necessary. In most cases, I would consider this to be a waste of time and money.

InDesign can export good validated ePUBs: fixed layout and reflowable. Some things are still missing, but they're not just missing from InDesign but from all WYSIWYG applications. This was because of one simple issue. In order to do simple things like text wraps (CSS: alignments), sidebars (CSS: divs), and all the rest, before CC 2014 you had to crack the compressed ePUB file and mess with its innards (many files and folders)

CS6 made major strides toward solving the text wrap and sidebar issues. CC has solved many more problems—CC2014 many more. However, it is still not clean and simple. Plus, there are many design issues which suggest that text wraps and sidebars do not work well in ebooks, regardless. The largest issue is how to handle a div or text wrap which crosses the border of a page break. If the reader changes the font or the size of the type, all the page breaks change also. The ereaders have no real way to handle a graphic or a sidebar which crosses a page break.

InDesign has become that simple program which allows you to do this visually—sort of. Anything more must be done on the code level and most of us are simply not ready to do that. It is possible to do the editing in Dreamweaver, but it is not pleasant and it is certainly not a good design experience. You are going to make some tough decisions about your ebooks. This is true no matter what you are using to format.

Bottom line: many things which are easily done in print, PDFs, and ePUB3 FXL are impossible in reflowable ePUBs or e-ink

Here are InDesign's abilities for the various versions

We will cover the details later in this book. However, I wanted to mention these here because so many people are trying to limp along with older versions.

InDesign CS5 and Earlier: have no real way to make ePUBs directly. The copy/paste into your HTML/CSS editor and code by hand method is your only real option.

InDesign CS5.5 can produce validated ePUBs: but your book layouts take a lot of work. The copy/paste into your HTML/CSS editor and code by hand method is the best option.

InDesign CS6 did quite a bit to write better code: but it still takes a lot of setup on your part. The ePUBs validate, but lists are compromised and embedded fonts do not work with the iBooks Store. The Amazon plug-in for CS6 does better Kindle books than InDesign does ePUBs. But the plug-in cannot handle nested styles, for example.

InDesign CC 2014 helps a lot: It validates and writes ePUBs with embedded fonts which upload fine through iTunes Producer. If you convert your lists to text upon export, lists work well. You can now add an index with active links. You can add a TOC anywhere with links to the anchors of the style in the TOC. This makes Lists for Graphics possible, for example. Plus, tables now are beginning to work well. This enables several layout solutions.

Anchored object control now works—except for inline objects. They must be anchored as Above Line or Custom. They can now float left or right and it works with a text wrap. Plus the text wrap will let you inset your floating objects from the edge of the column. All of this works with iBooks, most supposedly work with Kindle KF8 [but only if you own a Fire HD or better], and if you sell DRM-free versions from your Website or through Gumroad or Ganxy. Increasing portions work in more and more ereaders. InDesign's ePUBs convert very well with Amazon's free Kindle Previewer into KF8 books keeping everything until Amazon converts them again upon upload. A direct upload sometimes even keeps the embedded fonts in my Kindle apps for OSX and iOS.

 **Even drop cap graphics work well with CC reflowable ePUBs:** the major limitation left is that tall, narrow graphics get destroyed if the page break puts them partially on one page and partially on the next. I'm not sure what the solution is—other than using the break book before graphic setting. That often gives grotesque page breaks.

InDesign CC 2014 is finally a professional ePUB production tool: The largest advancement is the ability to produce Fixed Layout ePUBs. But, major advances have been made with reflowable ePUBs also. Tables now work fairly well with controls for stroke and fill—but no gradients yet. It is still very hard to get the width right also. A graphic will resize. Plus anchored graphics are now fairly predictable. The graphics now come in with the stroke and fill of the frame containing the graphic [without any gradients unless rasterized].

The ePUB limitations

Many of the excellent design possibilities of print are simply not available in ePUBs. What I intend to do is give you a list of changes you must make to get a validated ePUB. The good news is that several things that I would have had to mention for CS5.5 were no longer necessary for CS6 and even fewer are required for CC. Fixed layout ePUBs eliminate even more of the limitations.

Digital books are a very different world. You must rethink your concept of a book in order to design one which will work well for ePUBs and Kindle books. Let's talk about some of these necessary changes. But first:

Why are ebooks so different?

The most important factor is adjustable type: The reader controls font sizes globally and can override your font choices. At this point, even as a designer you get limited control over font choice, font style, font size, font spacing, or typography in general. These critical typographic concerns are downgraded to CSS2 capabilities—but with far fewer fonts even on the iPad. Obviously, this is one of the limitations of ePUB FXL. The bad news is that the reader can still override a lot of it [be it on their head].

Plus, there are other issues: OpenType features are not available. CSS2 can handle this, but no ereader I know of is capable. We are back to the very limited 256 character choices. As a reader, in most cases, you get maybe two fonts with up to four styles, a dozen sizes (maybe), and that's it. Often you only get one font family—especially with e-Ink ereaders like the early Kindles, Nook, and Kobo.

As a designer, unless you embed fonts, you get the number of fonts available (just serif and sans serif at best, unless you're on an iPad), four typestyles (regular, italic, bold, & bold italic), largely unlimited sizes & line spacing, alignments, indents & paragraph spacing, nested styles (or hand-applied character styles), a couple of list styles, all set up with p and the six headline styles [h1-h6] plus unlimited classes, and all of this directly out of InDesign. In most cases (except for old Kindles, Nooks, and Kobos plus their apps on desktops, iPads, iPhones, and Android machines) you are able to control the serif and sans serif choices.

The second major factor in reflowable ePUBs is the single column layout: Liquid Layout with its automatic column additions and graphic resizing and mask changes for various ereaders and smart phones has no real bearing on ePUBs. It's developed for use in InDesign's Digital Publishing System [DPS]. That is: app design for magazines with tablets—where multi-column pages are the norm. We are not there with ePUBs. There is just not enough width to display two columns or more except for landscape tablets. Even with fixed layout ePUBs, multiple columns are rendered so small that they are virtually unreadable. However, non-facing-page landscape designs should work fine with a great deal of care.

 As usual, this is changing as you read this: Currently, it is recommended that you embed fonts for KF8 [Kindle Fire], the iBooks Store, FXL on Kobo, and DRM-free versions sold directly to readers using a resource like Gumroad. InDesign CC embeds fonts well. If I email a copy with fonts to my iPad and open it in most of the ereaders, it works well. The embedded fonts remain and the anchored objects render correctly. But, many of the distributors cannot handle it: not NookPress, Draft2Digital, Lulu, or Smashwords. I'll post changes in these policies in *The Skilled Workman* as soon as I find new capabilities.

Many believe that fixed layout ePUBs are the answer, but they negate the fluidity and flexibility of an ebook. There is some hope. Adobe [December 2013] announced that they will be giving free licensing of their DPS format. Now it is theoretically possible to make an ereader or an app which can use DPS for books. But only time will tell.

It may be that PDFs are still a better choice than fixed layout ePUBs. There is a real hope that the CCNext version of InDesign will deal with more of this. Nonetheless, it is still a radical change in setup.

CHAPTER SEVEN

Ebook Design

Ebooks are like a different species. Of course, the basic difference is that you are reading on a screen instead of on paper. But it goes much further than that. There are many things which can be explained easily using typography in a printed book or ePUB FXL which are quite difficult to accomplish in a reflowable e-book. Conversely, except for the e-Ink ereaders, all ebooks are available in full color—whether or not you decide to use it.

So, we change how much? *Everything.*

It is obvious we must rethink our book designs: The real question is how much do we want to change in the conversion from print to ebook? The unavoidable answer, at present, is that we need a complete redo. This goes quite a bit beyond simple repurposing. If you are going to use fixed layout ePUBs you will need two different redesigns: FXL and Reflowable.

Designing for quicker repurposing: This can certainly be done. What it requires is a clear idea of what is going to be needed for the conversion. In order to make your ePUB look as good as possible we need to think reasonably about how to set up our documents so they can be converted quickly. So, your decisions about the use of styles within your book are very important when you set up your layout and formatting in your print books.

Everything must be controlled with styles

The major thing to understand is that HTML freaks out with paragraphs which are not formatted. All type must be controlled by paragraph styles, plus character styles as necessary. All graphics must be anchored and controlled with an object style. I haven't used the new table capabilities enough to have a definitive answer yet; but it is more than likely that table and cell styles are now necessary also.

The first e-book was the downloadable PDF in color

Scribd is a good example of a supplier which provides downloadable PDFs to their readers. But there are many more: Lulu, Gumroad, Ganxy, and hundreds of others [even though most specialize in free downloads and do not sell books]. Scribd, Gumroad, Ganxy, and Lulu are the main ones we are concerned with because they sell your PDFs.

The production of your color PDF should be very easy if you have followed my suggestions about graphics. If so, you have a Originals folder which has all of the graphics used in your book in full color with the same name. If not, it can take quite a while to find the originals.

Remember, PDFs can use printing quality graphics & vectors

So, all you have to do is package your completed book. This places a copy of your document into a new folder at the location of your choice. All of the linked graphics are copied to a new Links folder inside your new package. You should be able to drag a copy of your Originals folder to that same location. Then you can simply drag/drop the colored images into your Links folder. The grayscale images will be replaced by the color versions.

There are a few other things you should do for your downloadable PDFs. If your print book is normal, you will have a half title followed by a blank page before your title page. You should delete both of those and replace your title page image with a full bleed, full-color cover. You can move the Table of Contents to the back of the book because your PDF will have a complete set of bookmarks in the left column. You can put an internal link to take the reader to the beginning of the actual content. Other front matter should demonstrate a true benefit to the reader in the front or moved to the back of the book.

InDesign CC 2014 now exports fixed layout ePUBs [FXL]>>> !

I put the exclam on that because everyone else is so excited about this ability. It may turn out to be a big deal. It is essential for illustrated books like children's books. I'm not too excited. It's still not nearly as good as a PDF. **However:** the iBooks Store will sell an ePUB FXL, and that's really good. Kobo Writing Life also accepts one. Neither will sell a PDF. That's why I'm making this version of this book. Kindle KDP chews them up badly.

The pages look very much like they do in a PDF. You can do headers and footers, page numbers, paragraph rules, and excellent tables. It even handles gradient paragraph rules and gradient strokes and fills on the tables.

However, they are still ePUBs with no OpenType feature support, no true small caps, and so on. They also require Web graphics like all HTML documents—though, as mentioned, 150 dpi seems to work better. Some are pleasant surprises like the gradient strokes and fills within text blocks for rules & tables [they don't work for objects]. However, justified copy does not work. I'll cover the rules for FXL as I go through the changes necessary for ePUB export.

Ebook front matter

One of the first changes you should make for your readers is the elimination of as much front matter as possible. It is much harder to skip through such things in an ereader. This is also true with PDFs—even though they look very close to your printed version of the book—but normally without spreads.

Adding hyperlinks

One of the major differences with ebooks is the ability to use hyperlinks for your footnotes and references. The only problems will be companies like Apple which do not allow most links. Lulu does not allow links in ePUBs. Smashwords watches them closely. The rest of them only object if you have a link which goes to a competitor. Kobo doesn't like it if you have a book link to the Kindle store, for example. In a little twist for the new FXL option, a fixed layout ePUB can have links to objects, but no type links work yet. I imagine the next major upgrade will have them.

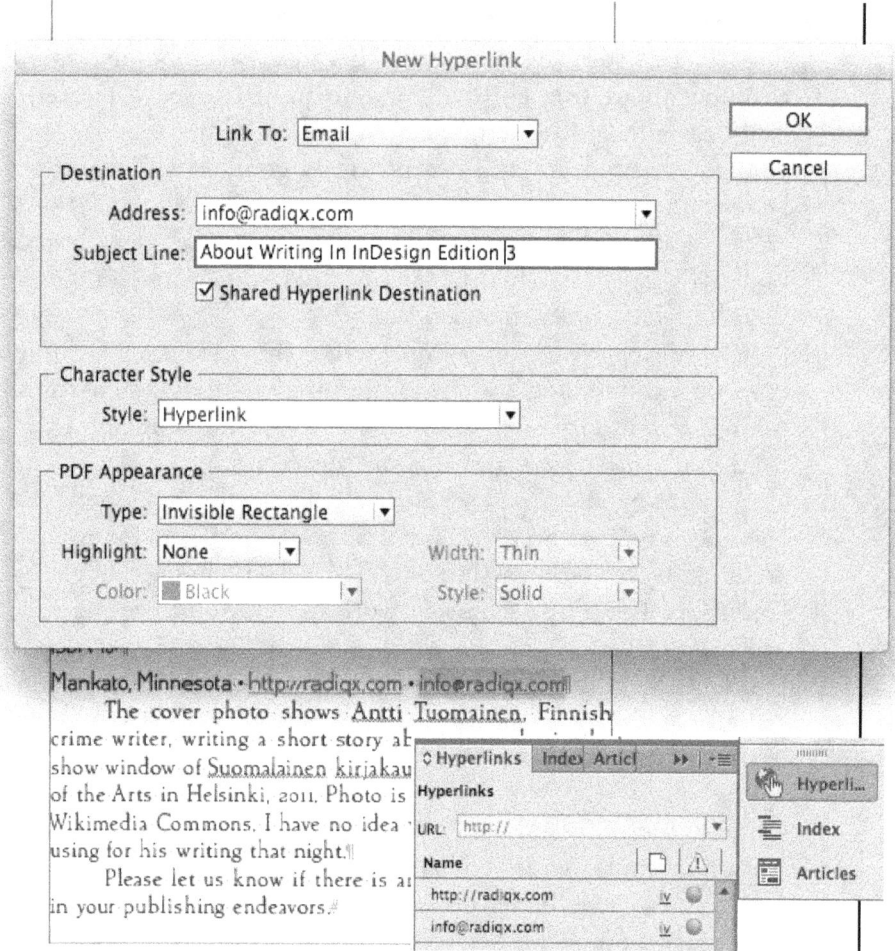

Adding hyperlinks is very easy. You use the Hyperlinks panel. As you can see above, you simply select what you want linked, open the New Hyperlink dialog, and paste in the URL. Or, in the case of the capture, type in the email address and add a subject line. You can easily add a character style for your linked text. If you do not, the default is usually a blue underline. I've tried special fonts and sizes, but that looks very contrived and artificial. The new Hyperlink shortcut is Command+7 in CC.

Contact info

It is very easy and necessary to add links to your email, FaceBook, Pinterest, Twitter account, and so on. You want your readers to be able to get in touch with you. This is one of the strongest advantages we have over traditional publishers.

Many authors and publishing houses delegate this to staff. That is not a good thing. The readers are looking for contact with the author or publisher. If you do end up with someone screening your email, make sure that personal requests are bounced directly to the author or person being sought out. This interaction with the readers is one of the great benefits of the new self-publishing paradigm.

Reflowable ePUB Design

With ePUBs we enter a whole new world. Normally this type of ebook is very fluid. Fonts and font size can easily be changed. Margins can be adjusted. Background colors can be stylized. The brightness can be adjusted to adapt to ambient conditions. You need to drop your preconceptions now!

At this point I am assuming that you have a finished and formatted book for print and probably a downloadable PDF. The question is how do we take this and convert it to an ePUB ebook and a Kindle version? This question has become more complex now that we have the fixed layout option to export ePUB FXL books.

Important announcement! *This is current as of July 2014*

This field of design is changing so rapidly that anything a month old is at least a bit out of date. The good news is that the methods I will cover here will still work. The bad news is that some may no longer be necessary.

I remember that it took from the late 1980s until the very late 1990s before desktop publishing for print even started to settle down—and then InDesign changed everything. Now I can say with confidence that print production has not advanced much at all since CS2 or CS3. You can easily use old versions of software for print production. This is not true for ePUBs and Kindle ebooks. You need InDesign CC 2014. The main problem is now ereader capabilities. This means you need to produce different versions: one reflowable ePUB with embedded fonts, one without, plus special versions for Smashwords & Kindle, possibly a fixed layout version, a downloadable PDF in color, and print.

Document size

At present for ePUBs I am using a document with a Web intent:
iPad vertical (768x1024 pixels), with 84 pixel margins right
and left; and 112 pixel margins top and bottom. This gives me
a Primary text frame of 600x800 which is nearly the maximum image size for an image in an ePUB on an iPad2. The
Retina resolution (double the iPad2) has no standardized
techniques yet. Nook and Kobo use the same width but
shorter images [Nook 760 tall and Kobo 600 square?]. I'll
cover Kindle later—but the Fire also likes 600x800 pages
though 600 x 500 images are preferred and a 127K file size is
rigidly enforced.

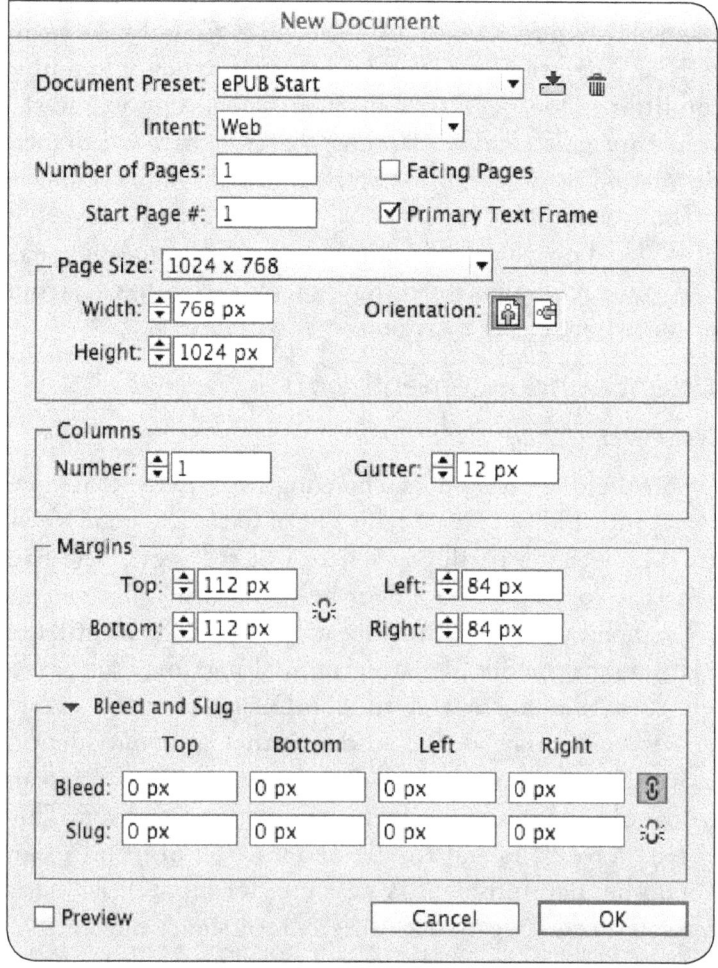

**You just have a single master page because you cannot use
page numbers, headers, or footers anyway [except in FXL]:**

Everything must be in a single story from the front page to the last word at the end. This is the old HTML page with infinite scrolling. It ain't purdy, but it's what we have to deal with. And you can do a lot. Now that we have anchored objects which can reliably float left or right with a text wrap, things have gotten a lot better. The only real issue is floating graphics which cross page breaks. You need to watch this very carefully. In actual practice, floating graphics much taller than 100 pixels will cause problems sooner or later. The problem is that floating graphics which cross page breaks are simply eliminated and the readers cannot see them at all.

Page sizing for fixed layout ePUBs

This is still in its infancy for me. The conceptual change is that you need to be working in an InDesign document where the page is easily readable on screen. You need to make sure your body copy is in the 9-12 words per line standard. I recommend using portrait half-letter up to 7" x 10". This one is set at 6" x8", so a 600x800 cover will work well. For landscape pages, I would shoot for the emerging HD standard: 960 pixels wide by 540 pixels tall. When I get a book that can use it, I'll be using 9.6" x 5.4" as a starting point. That should easily handle two columns.

Just remember, limitations are the birthing place for creative solutions.

This is always the case. The first thing you do when designing a book is determine the limitations: page size, fonts used, and so on. It's always something. Fixed layout ePUBs exported from InDesign can not display justified copy. This is due to what the InDesign engineers had to do to convert the page to a fixed layout retaining searchable type. However, the solution they came up with now means you can use paragraph rules and gradients.

Graphic format, size, and resolution

This one is rough for those of us accustomed to print quality—and that is almost everyone. Ereader graphics always look horrible when compared to print [except for the PDFs]. Even PDFs are stuck with screen resolution {though you can zoom into a vector graphic remarkably well]. What you basically need to understand is that you will be using relatively large Web graphics—but 72 dpi in most cases, not 300 dpi. This is obviously a serious conflict with the way we have been working for the past decade.

Basically you need JPEGs— a maximum of 600×800 pixel, RGB. For flat areas of color and sharp contrast, a GIF may look better. PNGs work also. You just need to make your choices in Photoshop's Save For Web dialog box. The Nook and Fire have different image size requirements as we'll see in a bit—especially the file size limits in Kindle.

 **Remember! Do not re-save JPEGs:** Every time you recompress an image as a JPEG, you add artifacts on top of the other artifacts. Work in PSD with multiple layers or TIFF and then save JPG, GIF, or PNG versions of the graphics for your various ebooks.

This obviously takes some planning ahead as you will be using grayscale images (vector PDFs if possible) in your print documents—in most cases. You'll have CMYK images if you print in color. These bitmapped images will be PSDs preferably, and TIFFs upon occasion. So from the beginning, as you write and create, you need to save RGB versions of your color images. You probably also want color versions of your PDF graphics for easy conversions. Then using Save For Web as a 100% JPEG will not noticeably ruin the image.

At this point, even though the ePUB3 spec accepts SVG, which is a vector form of graphic, none of the ereaders do—with the possible exception of Kindle Fire and books produced with Apple's iBooks Author. InDesign cannot handle SVG images now, regardless.

From what I have heard recently, SVG will not work for what we need. But others have said that's not true, SVG will meet our needs. Regardless, we need vector images for ebooks, and they are not available. Out side of InDesign users, no one seems to care.

Reflowable graphics MUST be to size and not cropped: Graphics must be placed at 100% and fit the frame proportionally without cropping. If not, your exported ePUBs will ignore the graphic. There can also be no corner effects, dropped shadows or anything like that. All these things work fine in fixed layout but not at all in Reflowable.

Everything in one story for reflowable

For reflowable ePUBs, you must remember the image of an eternally scrolling Web page. That is truly what we are dealing with. Of course, we want things like sidebars, inset text wraps, and so on. They work well in HTML. With certain limitations, InDesign CC 2014 can now export them for us. But the limitations are caused by the code needed

The problem isn't with the ePUB standard

The problem is with the ereader hardware and tablet apps available to read what we publish. I read my ePUBs in iBooks on my iPad. They look so much better than is possible in the old Kindles, Kobo, or Nook. I know that purchasers of my ePUBs and Kindle books will be stuck with much less. An ePUB is a new capability [way less than a decade]. All I have to do is remember how limited PageMaker 4.2 and Quark 3 were when I began in digital publishing in 1991. Right now KF8 on the Kindle Fire or the Readium Chrome extension is best for Android devices, and iBooks on the new iPad are best for type and graphics. Overall, iBooks is probably the best ereader available. I realize that many are still deeply tied to their e-Ink Kindles, Kobos, & Nooks. [Beware! Think dodo bird. Some will be extinct soon.]

Eliminate all separate stories [reflowable]

Remember that everything in an ePUB must be in one story or in a div attached to it floating above line, right, or left. This is a radical conversion in many cases. And you will need to do much of it by hand. The Articles Panel is a help, but in my experience it takes longer to order things in this way and it is certainly not a flawless conversion.

So, I drag'n'drop any separate stories into an inline location that makes sense—rewriting as necessary to keep the copy flowing well. Again, simply repurposing is not a good idea. ePUBs are a very different reading experience and we must adapt to it.

What I find is concepts which can be easily shown with typography in a PDF are completely lost in an ePUB—even a fixed layout ePUB. I commonly need to rewrite copy to deal with this fact. Type within an anchored sidebar usually needs to be rewritten and placed into a different location to make sense as a part of the one story. Often, all text sidebars must be simply eliminated. Plus, OpenType features don't work.

Live type in an anchored frame now works: BUT, you need to be very careful. The rewraps are very different. The apparent file size is often larger. And in general, they simply do not look good. You can get borders and flat color backgrounds, but gradients haven't made it yet [except in FXL]. You cannot use a gradient in live type, at present. But I have to believe that the talented engineers on the InDesign team are working toward that.

Easily converted anchored graphics:

For very graphic books like mine with the wrapped graphics, I simply redo the object style for the graphics so that it drops them in Above Line or Custom locations. Moving graphics around to make the most sense becomes easy with the new drag'n'drop anchoring controls built into the frame edge—upper side, right corner. Simply drag them into position and convert them to the object style of your choice with a shortcut. I make many of my graphic conversions 600 pixels wide, because I want them as large as they can be to help you actually read them. But I have had to reduce the width [upping the resolution to 150 dpi] for this ePUB FXL version.

Wrapped graphics are definitely doable. They can float left or right and the indent can be controlled by the outside text wrap, which becomes the margin. The biggest missing capability is in setting sizing with percentages. Now, all you can do is set the pixel width. But the Tip icon in the next paragraph here is simply floated left, with a text wrap on the left side of 28.8 pixels [the same as my first line indent] for my reflowable version. Here it's float right. But that only works in iBooks and iPad's version of the BlueFire ereading app. You'll get sick of all the ereader variations. However, each of the suppliers sells to a different group of people

Dealing with captions: Supposedly, they are grouped with the graphic and then set off with an Object style. I've had trouble getting the live text to work because it changes size with

the rest of the text, and the graphic would need to be a grouped Object. That now works, I'm told.

The Object Style controls

The new Export Options: in the Object Style dialog are pretty self-explanatory. You have three choices: Alignment & Spacing, Float Left, and Float Right. As you can see below, you can control left, right, center alignment plus spacing before and after. The only strange thing is that Inline will not work for your Anchored Object Settings. It must be Above Line or Custom. If you leave it inline, no matter what it is, it will be re-rasterized and the result will be a mess.

Setting the text wrap will translate to the margins of the div inserted. So, I may need to adjust the text wrap a few times to get everything to line up as needed by my design. In

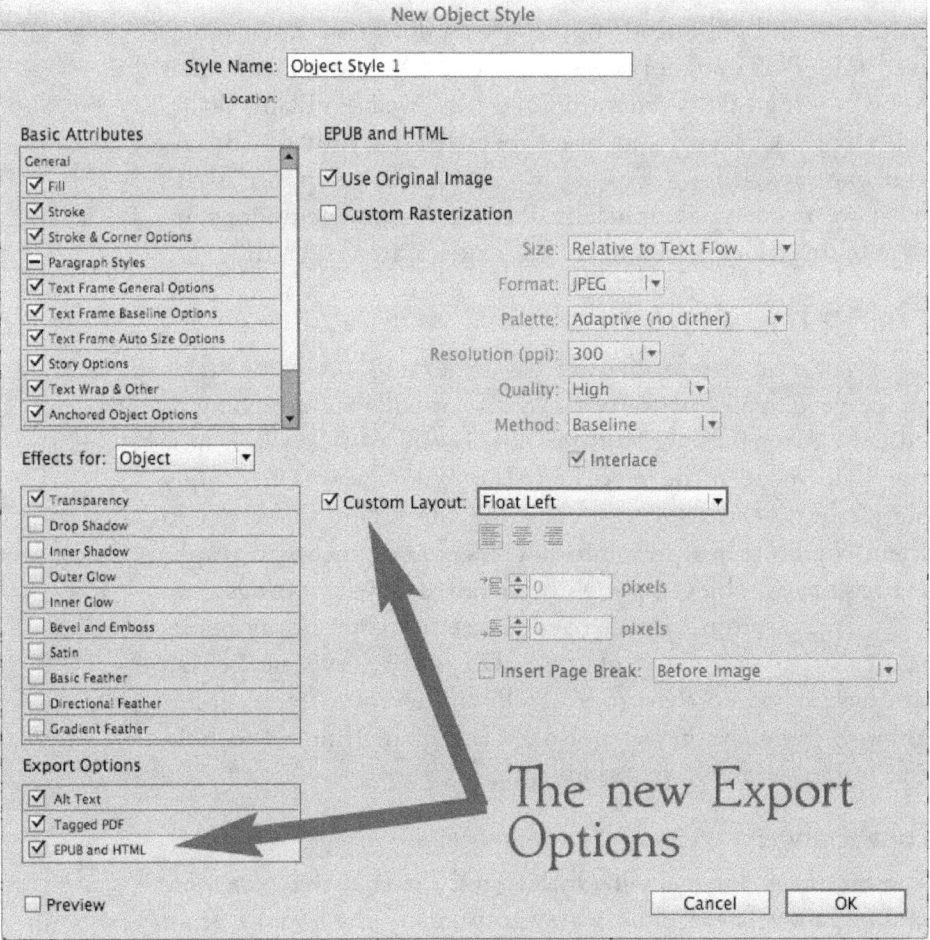

print and in a downloadable PDF, I commonly locally format these problems. I did that for the previous capture. But that doesn't work in reflowable ePUBs.

Be patient with all of this. Adding ebooks to the publishing repertoire is a very complex operation for Adobe. InDesign CC 2014 is a major step upward toward a more stable, more usable, more easily exportable ePUB. InDesign CCNext version (six months or so from now) will do even better. We have been assured by Adobe that ePUB3 is very high on their priority list. In fact, we know they joined Readium (hopefully to add ePUB3 capabilities to ereaders).

Adobe has a good reputation of bringing these things online—and for doing it better than we expected. I know I certainly did not expect Liquid Layout, yet we got that for CS6. It may only apply to magazines at this point, but ePUB3 will probably use it more—both in InDesign and in ereaders. The iPad, Fire, and Kobo read simple ePUB3 docs now. Kobo promised full ePUB3 support by spring 2013. FXL works with their Kobo Writing Life, I cannot upload a reflowable ePUB3 yet.

For CC 2014, I did not expect fixed layout ePUBs. As you know, what I am looking for is full CSS2 support. That's what we need typographically. But the fashion lemmings are demanding video and audio. The readers aren't—AFAIK.

Fixing the styles

For ease of reformatting, we use exactly the same styles as we developed for print or FXL. Eventually we are going to edit the exported tags. But for now I want to talk about how the styles need to be modified. The easiest way is to simply start editing the copy and changing the styles as we get to them. We must bear in mind that sidebars or anchored graphics require an object style with anchored object settings.

Again, often I find I need to rewrite copy in my books to deal with the reality of the ePUB reading experience. Do not hesitate to do that. Your ePUB will have a different ISBN anyway, if you bother to get one. The main thing is to help the reader as much as possible.

Font changes

The big news, for me, with InDesign CC is that they can now embed fonts: These ePUBs are accepted by the iBooks Store

& Kindle Previewer. To do that, you'll need an iTunes Connect account and upload things on the Mac. You have to encrypt the fonts to embed them. But the finished ePUBs upload fine through iTunes Connect. The fixed layout ePUBs with embedded fonts work fine in Kobo Writing Life. Eventually, this will be commonplace and InDesign is leading the way. They really help readability if used carefully.

Corinthian Light

ABCDEFGHIJKLMNOPQ
RSTUVWXYZ1234567890
abcdefghijklmnopqrstuvwxyz

Created by Letraset Type Director Colin Brignall, this clean-cut, monolineal sans serif typeface was inspired by Edward Johnston's Railway Type and Eric Gill's Gill Sans typefaces. *Myfonts*

Defining typography

* **Webster's:** The craft of composing type and printing from it; art and technique of printing with movable type.

* **Random House:** the art or process of printing with type; the work of setting and arranging types and of printing from them; the general character or appearance of printed matter

* **Cambridge:** the style, size and arrangement of the letters in a piece of printing

* **Wikipedia:** art of arranging letters on a page to be printed, usually for a combination of aesthetic and functional goals

What's unusual is ... really get it. They ... typography really has ... of arranging letters on ...

Obviously physica... shapes play a huge role in type design. But typography goes far beyond the actual shapes into cultural and

Embedded fonts
Readium or
iBooks

Corinthian Light

ABCDEFGHIJKLMNOPQ
RSTUVWXYZ1234567890
abcdefghijklmnopqrstuvwxyz

Created by Letraset Type Director Colin Brignall, this clean-cut, monolineal sans serif typeface was inspired by Edward Johnston's Railway Type and Eric Gill's Gill Sans typefaces. *Myfonts*

Defining typography

Webster's: The craft of composing type and printing from it; art and technique of printing with movable type.

Random House: the art or process of printing with type; the work of setting and arranging types and of printing from them; the general character or appearance of printed matter

Cambridge: the style, size and arrangement of the letters in a piece of printing

Wikipedia: art of arranging letters on a page to be printed, usually for a combination of aesthetic and functional goals

What's unusual is that none of the dictionaries really get it. They describe the physical act, but typography really has little to do with the physical act of arranging letters on paper for ...

Obviously physical consideratio... in type design. But typography g... cultural and subjective responses ... the

No fonts embedded
Kindle Mac App

Even though the ePUB spec says we can embed fonts, this is still spotty—not because it is difficult, but the ereader support is usually missing. It is also difficult to find a place to upload an ebook with embedded fonts which is acceptable. Lulu, Nook Press, Kobo Writing Life, Draft2Digital, and Smashwords still reject the ePUBs which use them. They consider these ePUBs to be encrypted. But Kobo takes fixed layout ePUB3 books which do have embedded fonts. So, the support for ePUB3 seems to matter a lot.

My current recommendation is to embed fonts for iBooks and choose fonts that are available on the iPad for the non-embedded version. Of course, PC users will have some trouble with that. For the Fire and Fire HD, we can embed fonts but you must make sure that you are using fonts with the proper licensing. You can also read embedded font ePUBs in BlueFire on the iPad [usually]. Font producers like me can use their own, but you'll have a hard time finding a supplier who sells ePUB rights. However, TypeKit , which comes with your CC subscription, offers several hundred fonts with an ePUB license.

I want to mention the iPad fonts

With iOS6 or better, the iPad supports 60 font families: If you do not have fonts with an ebook license for embedding, the iOS font set is the best available. But you cannot embed them. They will give you good serif and sans serif tags for your ePUBs without embedded fonts. So, they can be used to help produce your styles for non-embedded versions. In fact, until the other distributors can accept embedded fonts, I use ePUBs with the styles asking for fonts available on the iPad. That way my uploads to distributors like Draft2Digital can sell ePUBs through iBooks with decent typography.

However, TypeKit gives CC owners plenty of good fonts to embed!

The main thing for us, in this book, is to have a little discussion about what will work and what will not for your ePUBs. Font choices are always a highly personal thing. I'm going to suggest my personal tastes and give you reasons. You make up your own mind. You can use the fonts I use in this book. I'll sell them to you cheap. Go to *The Skilled Workman* and look at the Fonts page to find some publishing font packages I am selling at very good pricing.

Verboten fonts [Courier]

First, I'm just going to mention the ugly ones you should never use: Courier or New Courier. These eight fonts should never be used unless you are trying to evoke a period, make a historical statement, or something strange. But almost everyone believes they are hideous fonts (not to mention they are very difficult to read).

Fonts with bad reader reactions [TIMES & ARIAL]

These fonts are not bad designs, but they have issues—some of them fatal. I don't use them.

- **Arial:** This font family with dozens of styles is the ugly cousin of Helvetica used to avoid the royalties. As far as I know, Microsoft had it designed precisely for that reason. These fonts plus Times make up the core of some of the most overused fonts in existence. Plus they are the default for many bureaucracies.

- **Times New Roman & Times:** These families normally have regular, italic, bold and bold italic. Though the bold pairs tend to be too narrow and ugly with plugged counters, the real problem is the bureaucratic associations. Times always brings up strong negative emotions for most people. At best, it looks like a book designed in Word. This is why this tends to be the font family of choice for many authors. Just think "non-professional" to help with your cure.

Bureaucratic fonts: These are the fonts that have been the defaults in Office, Publisher, and similar non-professional page layout tools for decades—Arial, Times, and Times Roman. They are not very pretty fonts. The true situation is that non-professionals who use nothing but software defaults are the only people who use these fonts. In fact, most bureaucracies have standardized them and require their use. The only books to use them are those using Word conversions.

They trigger our bureaucratic drivel filter.

For example, if you watch yourself when you open your mail or when you receive handouts, you will see that bureaucratic output is quickly consigned to the trash—usually without being read. Most people are fully aware that there is no usable content in these things. Bureaucratic output is produced purely to prove to administrators that something was done—even though we all know that nothing was done except some committee meetings. Our experience tells us these are usually a waste of time to read. Most of us throw them away unread (unless, of course, we are a member of the dratted committee).

So also, almost everyone simply tosses mail with obvious Word output without reading it—consigning it to the junk mail category in their mind automatically. Beyond that, default Word or Publisher output is barely readable. The default typography settings are very bad and obvious. There are simply too many really bad associations with these fonts to use them.

Versatile fonts for typography

The basic point is simple: You want to choose fonts that read well, have matching x-heights [if you use run-ins], and which will make the distinction between serif and sans serif in the CSS exported with the ePUB.

iOS7 gives us several quite good choices here. I also want to mention some of the standards included in Type-Kit. These are font families that are relatively easy to read and comfortable for the reader. There are several fine serif choices, and many sans serif families. There are enough choices for you to be able to make your ePUBs unique, stylish and very readable.

For body copy you need at least regular, bold, and italic styles for your typographic needs. A bold italic is nice—but not often needed. You'll need these fonts installed on your machine to use them in InDesign. TypeKit allows you to embed the CC fonts into your ePUBs.

I used to follow this paragraph with the complete listing of iOS fonts. But that no longer seems useful. The iBooks conundrum is one that I haven't quite figured out yet. It definitely does the best job of presenting your ePUBs with support for embedded fonts, floating divs, and anything that InDesign can export. However, the iBooks Store does not sell books I upload directly very well. Books uploaded through Smashwords and Draft2Digital sell much better through the iBooks Store than the versions I upload directly through iTunes Connect and iTunes Producer.

It is quite frustrating—if I allow myself to think about it. I would like to get beyond my dependence upon Amazon, but no one else offers the capabilities of Amazon either for book discovery or for ebook display. PLus, amazon is commony the cheapest. The only lack is Amazon's poor support of its iPad and OSX apps.

So, what I want to do is simply suggest some font combinations that should work well for you. In the full *Writing In InDesign CC 2014 Producing Book* I have a fairly large section on using a companion sans for your serif font. I said there that finding a good pair which works well together is difficult. In fact, it is nearly impossible. I finally gave up and designed my own—the Contenu/Buddy pair I am using in this book.

Ebook standards are different

People who read ebooks are a new breed. Many of them are, like myself, shall we say mature. A decent percentage of the new readers using ereaders are in their 50s or higher. We tend to like traditional typesetting, because that is what we are used to. However, even here there are some new trends we need to be aware of as designers.

In ebooks, I have seen several postings suggesting that non-fiction should be done with sans serif body copy. I would be very careful about that, but there is certainly no reason why you cannot choose a truly humanist sans like Optima or even Gill Sans for your body copy. Be sure that you pick one that is very readable. Then you can use elegant serif faces for your heads and get a beautiful book. I suspect that my next font design will be a readable sans to match with an elegant display serif.

Plus, the reader of your reflowable ebooks can change fonts at will: Reflow is the goal. That trumps typography in an ebook. Also remember, that a reflowable ePUB on an iPad, or converted to KF8 for the Fire, is the typographic wonder of the ebook world—as are fixed layout ePUBs on Kobo and iBooks. All the other ereaders support reflowable ePUBs without embedded fonts. This is true for the many android tablets with apps. But without embedded fonts the font options remain abysmal.

According to an article on ireaderreview.com the following fonts are available on the older ereaders and 'droid tablets. You quickly see that the iPad and iPhone give us exceptional choices. The Kindle Fire is certainly headed in that direction by supporting embedded fonts, but the Kindle apps often do not. So things are indeed getting better, but only in slow, incremental steps.

- **Kindle uses PMN Caecilia a condensed version of Caecilia, and a sans serif option:** this is a very readable slab serif but I haven't found out what the sans serif is.

- **Nook uses Helvetica Neue (sans-serif), Amasis (serif), and Light Classic (serif):** Amasis is a more humanist slab serif.

- **Kobo seems to have 7 typefaces:** Amasis, Avenir, Delima, Felbridge, Georgia, Gill Sans and Rockwell.

- **Android OS has three font families:** Droid Sans, Droid Sans Mono and Droid Serif and this includes the Nook Tablet and Kindle Fire.

The Kindle, Nook, and Kobo, choices may be easily readable on their e-ink devices. But they certainly do not provide good typographic choices for a designer.

Your only real font choices are serif or sans, plus you can add italic and bold: The problem, of course, is that serif or sans were not a font choice in InDesign 5.5 or earlier. The good news is that InDesign CS6 and better adds those choices automatically when you export to ePUB. The bad news is that many of the ereaders simply ignore any meaningful font instructions.

However, we must remember the ebooks using the currently limited choices are selling like crazy. Kindle still has a majority of the overall market, but the iBooks Store is growing rapidly as the iPad becomes the dominant tablet for ereading. If you want to sell to that market, you need to make a book that fits their paradigm. In my case, non-fiction about InDesign and font design sell about twice as much on Kindle as they do on iBooks (but print is still better than a third of sales). Nook and Kobo are still negligible (for me). These percentages will continue to change regularly as the market matures.

Amazon is still over half of my sales. They seem to be slowly slipping. The domination of Amazon has run its course for me. I have heard others saying that Amazon's sales are going down. I suspect that will increase. Kobo is really making a push—as is the iBooks Store. Now that iBooks is available in OSX, I suspect iBooks will grow a lot. But everything is still controlled by the ebook distributors. One of these days that problem will be solved. At least I hope it will.

The problem is that most excellent text fonts for body copy have fairly small x-heights and there are not many sans serifs with x-heights that small. So, the only font sets you are likely to have is Lapture/Calluna Sans, Sirba/Effra, or other large x-height combinations. Now you can see why I created Buddy. A small x-height sans is essential for Garamond, Caslon, and so on. Otherwise we're the victims of fashion.

This is a worthwhile place to spend some time and money getting a usable family pairing you like.

Some Sample font pairs

❦ Contenu, Athelas, Garamond/Buddy

❦ Lapture/Calluna Sans

❦ Sirba/Effra

But enough on fonts.

Let's get back to ePUB design possibilities. These options get better all the time.

Size & Leading changes

We have quite a bit of control here. In an ePUB the font sizing and spacing must be specified in ems or pixels. InDesign is doing it in ems in CS6 & better [5.5 not so much]. Basically, 12 point type is converted to one em. Leading is converted to a multiple of that em. On the iPad's high resolution screen, one em is actually 16 pixels high (I guess that's 32 pixels for the Retina).

For fixed layout: you may well need to increase your point size to get an appropriate number of words per line.

Alignment

This was never a problem until CC 2014. But now **fixed layout ePUBs cannot handle justified copy**. So, you must be sure to convert any style which justifies the copy. It's a hassle, but it's a result of the coding process used as I mentioned earlier.

Small Caps & All Caps

Of course, because OpenType features do not work, true small caps are very rare. So, any typographically excellent true small caps would have to be in fonts that have them like Copperplate & Bodoni 72 Small Caps. The Open-Type variants will not be picked up. In the subhead before this paragraph, I am using small caps in the print and PDF versions. But here in an ePUB, the CAPS are in 15 point and the lowercase is in 12 point type. I set MALL and APS in a smaller point size [using a character style, but you will see they are much lighter] for my ePUBs and KF8 variants. Otherwise they would still not work in most ereaders. Even this workaround is commonly stripped out in the e-ink ereaders.

No special fonts: CONVERT TO GRAPHIC

If you need a special font, you need to make it into a graphic [unless you can embed it]. For fixed layout, embedded fonts are the norm so this is not an issue.

It would seem that selecting the words and choosing Create Outlines would do it. But the resulting rasterized graphic will be a bad size and very pixelated. Normally, it is necessary to make a separate PDF graphic with that type to rasterize into Photoshop. Then save as a Web graphic and place into your ePUB document. You will be doing this a lot—at least until the ereaders & distributors accept SVG or other vector files.

Remember: Embedded fonts have many legal issues. You need to be careful which fonts you use. Though you can embed any font you have on your computer in OTF or TTF formats—there are two major problems. In many cases, you will need to pay extra for an ePUB license. So, if there is any doubt (and believe me there is), do not embed fonts unless you are sure you own the rights and that it will look good. You can go to the bergsland.org site and click on the page Fonts for the fonts I am currently selling for ebook production. Plus, The TypeKit fonts with the Creative Cloud are designed for this.

Lists [fixed well in CC2014]

Lists do not translate well. HTML makes bad lists. For HTML lists, all you can do is delete all special indents you set up. Make it a numbered or bulleted list (with no special bullet) and let InDesign do the translation. It is not good. Remove all indents, left and right from lists unless you have

InDesign CC. However, the numbering of HTML lists will not continue to separated paragraphs.

For CC 2014: This problem is pretty much solved.

For reflowable ePUBs, it does quite well by using the "Convert To Text" option in the ePUB export dialog. For fixed layout, anything goes except OpenType glyphs.

Eliminate fancy bullets: FROM LISTS

Prior to CC [specifically InDesign CC 9.2] this was a real problem. You had to crack the ePUB and change the CSS to use special bullets—from the limited CSS choices. BUT NOW, you can use any character in the basic 256 like the delta, lozenge, and so on. The problem is that in the basic fonts, those characters are not very good choices.

For CC 2014: fancy bullets work well

In CC, if you use convert list to text, this option embeds bullets with special fonts [including dingbats] when converting to text, but only out of the basic 256 characters. The extra OpenType glyphs are not available. You can also make a Character Style with color and size changes to bulk up the bullets a wee bit.

Because I design my own fonts, I simply added some characters to use for bullets into my 256-character ebook font family.

Add chapter breaks with a H1 style

You must set up a H1 style (usually your headline) and specify it as the chapter break. Have it go to next page [not next odd page]. However, for iBooks, you can't do that either because it will add an extra blank page. The good news is that even with H1 setup without the Next Page Keeps control, CC ePUBs still maintain the page controls and move H1 paragraph to the top of the next page.

Eliminate all soft returns.

A soft return is a line break in a paragraph without adding a new paragraph [Alt+Enter on PC or Shift+Return on a Mac]. You will get rid of all of them when exporting a reflowable ePUB. But understand, soft returns are a real problem when the reader can change fonts and font sizes at will while he or she is reading. If you must do a line break, you may well be stuck with special paragraph styles with no space between paragraphs to make it work. Soft returns seem to work fine with fixed layout ePUBs. Just make sure you proof your ePUBs carefully.

Eliminate all OpenType feature use

Nothing can be done about this. Current ebook readers do not support OpenType features—yet. However, they probably will. It is part of the CSS2 scenario and therefore usable in the ePUB standard. This is a major change when moving from print and PDF to ePUB and Kindle books.

Eliminate tabular layouts

HTML/CSS does not support tabs so you'll need to use tables. Tables now work fairly well. And there is good reason to believe they'll be even better in the next version

Use tables [FXL: good; reflowable: eh OK]

InDesign 5.5 will export the tables, but they will look bad with all borders and backgrounds deleted or changed. CS6 does better and HTML/CSS can produce good tables, but no gradient fills, borders, or padding. **For reflowable ePUBs,** you will often want to set up a separate InDesign doc for the table, export a print PDF, and rasterize that in Photoshop as wide as is possible [normally 600 pixels]. However in CC 2014, regional cell styles are supported. Those are the choices seen in the capture below. These choices are on the General page to the Table Style Dialog. CC 2014 also supports strokes, fills, and padding. Rules are limited to solid, dotted, and dashed. A quirk: A border color of [None} maps to [Black] .

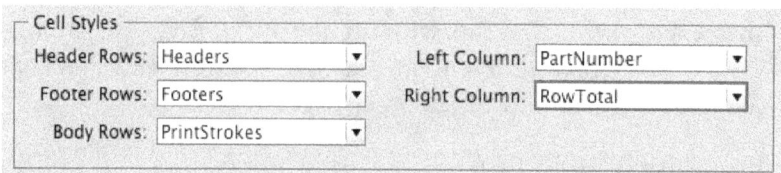

Tables in Fixed Layout ePUBs

Here the problem is solved. So far, everything I've tried has worked flawlessly in my fixed layout ePUBs: gradient borders and fills, any rule style [wavy line, triple line, or anything], and basically any table you do for a PDF works for an ePUB FXL.

Eliminate paragraph rules for reflowable

For the reflowable ePUBs, the only rules you have available are Underline and Strikethrough: without any customizing allowed. If you need the rules, you can create graphics that you can place before and/or after your paragraphs. The only problem with that is the difficulty with spacing control. Plus there is no way to do an overlap so you cannot have a rule as a bar from which the type reverses out to white. On the other hand, we are able to use simple tables with solid borders. You just need to test and see what works. Be prepared to change to use the new capabilities as they appear.

Fixed Layout ePUBs do paragraph rules well: You can do white or colored type over a gradient rule. You can even extend your rules outside the text frame. The only quibble I found was that these rules are cut off at the text frame border unless there is also a graphic out in that sidebar area as you see.

GRAPHICS IN INDESIGN CC FIXED LAYOUT 64

InDesign's forte is graphic assembly

The whole procedure I just described took less than a minute—real time. Well, actually, two minutes because I was careful to set the type well. So, I was able to copy/paste a complex drawing into editable paths in InDesign in less than a minute. Obviously, getting editable pieces from Illustrator is quick and easy.

Paragraph Rule

Using the brushstroke as a frame

To make a radical change, I modified the size of the circle to overlap the brushstroke, and pasted a picture of my home into the circle. This took another minute—with the result seen above. I added the type on top in another 20-30 seconds [the only glitch was that I had to set the new text frame to ignore text wraps as I had put a text wrap on the graphic automatically when I styled it with an object style] Regardless, the whole thing was done in far less time than it took to write this explanation. It is dramatic if not too inspiring.

A Minnesota winter at home!

If I wanted a graphic I could use anywhere: All I would need to do is copy and paste the new graphic onto a new single page document, save it, and export it as a PDF [which I did] If you are looking at this in an ebook, you can see it is in glorious 600-pixel-wide RGB color—rasterized in Photoshop and exported as a JPEG. For the B&W book, I could have rasterized into Photoshop and saved as a Grayscale PSD at 300 dpi.

You can do graphics like this very quickly. If you have the pieces at hand, any graphic of this nature can be done in less than a minute. Fancy tables with inserted photos and complex typography can be created in a separate document and exported as a PDF to be used wherever needed at whatever size you need.

Eliminate borders

You can use borders as a stroke on an object: But it depends on your version. For CS5.5, to add a border to a paragraph or group of paragraphs you need to edit the HTML and often add a div in the code. For CS6, you can add a stroke, fill, and corner options to your frames holding your graphics. InDesign still rasterizes them into graphics, but at least the look is there. For CC 2014, strokes almost work as expected, but only solid, dotted, and dashed. However, proof carefully. For CC 2014: This problem is pretty much solved.

Type color

You can make your type any color except gradients. You'll want to use RGB mixes.

CS5.5 & better now works with nested styles

Prior to 5.5, we had to hand format any character styles by selecting the type and applying the style. Now you can use nested styles in your ePUBs. In the exported ePUB they are converted to spans which you can control with the Export Tags dialog. The only fly in the ointment was that the Kindle Export Plug-In did not support nested styles.

 **The Kindle plug-in did not handle nested styles for CS6 & earlier:** Because I tend to do my Kindle books first, I was still converting all the automated nested styles into hand-formatted character styles.

However, for CC I am going back to nested styles. I recently dropped the use of the Amazon Kindle Export Plug-In in favor of making a special ePUB for Kindle [more on that in a bit] and then opening the ePUB in Kindle Previewer which will compile the ePUB into a Kindle KF8 archive. That worked fine, but lately I have just been uploading the ePUBs directly in KDP.

If you convert your KF8 books from an ePUB with Kindle Previewer most of this information survives, Kindle books are really frustrating. Sometimes you'll be sure you have it figured out and then the next day it won't work again. You may need to buy a Kindle for proofing.

Pages & master pages

Reflowable ePUBs: these are irrelevant as there are no pages in a reflowable ePUB.

Fixed layout ePUBs: Because they do pages, master pages with automatic page numbers work well. You can see an example of master page automatic page numbering in the capture from the fixed layout ePUB on the previous page and above in this document.

Making these changes & proofing

What needs to be done now is to go through all the styles used in your print document and convert them to work within ePUB limitations. Then export your ePUB and open it in Readium [in Chrome] and in iBooks. For Nook & Kobo, I email the ePUB to my iPad and open it in the readers. ADE2 will show you how bad it will look in the other ereaders,

BUT it will show your fonts in the desktop computer which has the fonts installed. That will not happen in the ereaders. You can set the export options to automatically open your ePUB in your best ereading app after it is exported.

If you own an iPad , Nook , and / or Kobo: open the ePUB in it to see how it will look there. They all have procedures to side-load ePUBs. Email it to yourself and open it from the email into the reader(s) of your choice with the iPad. It is especially important to check out the graphics and see how they fit. Adjust spacing as well as you possibly can. Be very careful to look for issues which work well in print and PDFs, but do not translate well to HTML—like soft returns, OpenType feature use, and so on.

If you are typographically trained and visually sensitive, this first attempt at an ePUB will be a horrible shock

The typographic ugliness of HTML after you have so carefully crafted your typography in your printed and fixed layout book is a major hit to the senses. Your ebook readers [the ones who buy your books] will not be shocked. But, there is no kerning or tracking, and spacing is very crude. All of your OpenType features will be gone. All the controls are very crude—displayed on a low resolution screen—when compared to print quality. But many of the new tablets have 300+ dpi resolution for checking graphics.

Take a deep breath! Now get on with it

You've learned to deal with this level of quality with Websites. *[If you haven't—shame on you!]* This is the reality of ePUB. Now your goal is to make it as easy to read as possible. It is likely that your first attempts will require you to fix several of your styles. Thankfully, they control the entire document globally because everything is formatted with no local formatting. This is one of the reasons why the use of styles is so critical.

Deal with reality

Do not hang on to impossible requirements. The more simple you make your typography the better it will work in this greatly restricted environment. There is nothing wrong with ePUB and the ePUB standard. It is simply different and requires a new sense of design. As InDesign improves we will have more control. The largest hurdle at this point, and for the near future, is ereader capabilities.

ePUB does give us much more

If we quit looking at ePUBs from the background of the printed book and start looking from the background of ebooks, then we can see how much we have available in an ePUB. Just focus on readability. If your readers have to work at reading your book, they'll try changing the size—but more likely they'll just quit reading.

Setting chapter breaks

This is a very important part of setting up your styles. Reflowable ePUBs do not support page breaks—with one exception. If you have a style set up as a headline, set up to start on the next page, the ePUB will start a new chapter when you use that paragraph style. But you must choose it when you export the ePUB. You find this choice in the ePUB Export Options dialog box: Break Document at Paragraph Style with a popup menu to pick the style.

 **New to CC:** The set up just mentioned above no longer works for books set up to upload to the iBooks Store. For them you need to leave Keeps set to Anywhere, and then check the style to Break in the Export All Tags Dialog. This gives the page break without an extra blank page.

Setting the TOC (THIS IS REQUIRED)

You do need to set up a TOC (Layout>> Table of Contents). You will chose this Table of Contents style in the ePUB Export dialog. The styles you choose for your TOC will be added to the bookmarks in the column to the left of your ePUB. You do not use leaders or page numbers as leaders do not work and page numbers do not exist in ebooks [more accurately the page numbers would change all time with reader changes to fonts and/or type size].

Keep the TOCs simple. They can quickly get very unwieldy in ebooks of any kind. If you are going to show them with links to the content locations, make them even more simple. Be concerned about the reading experience.

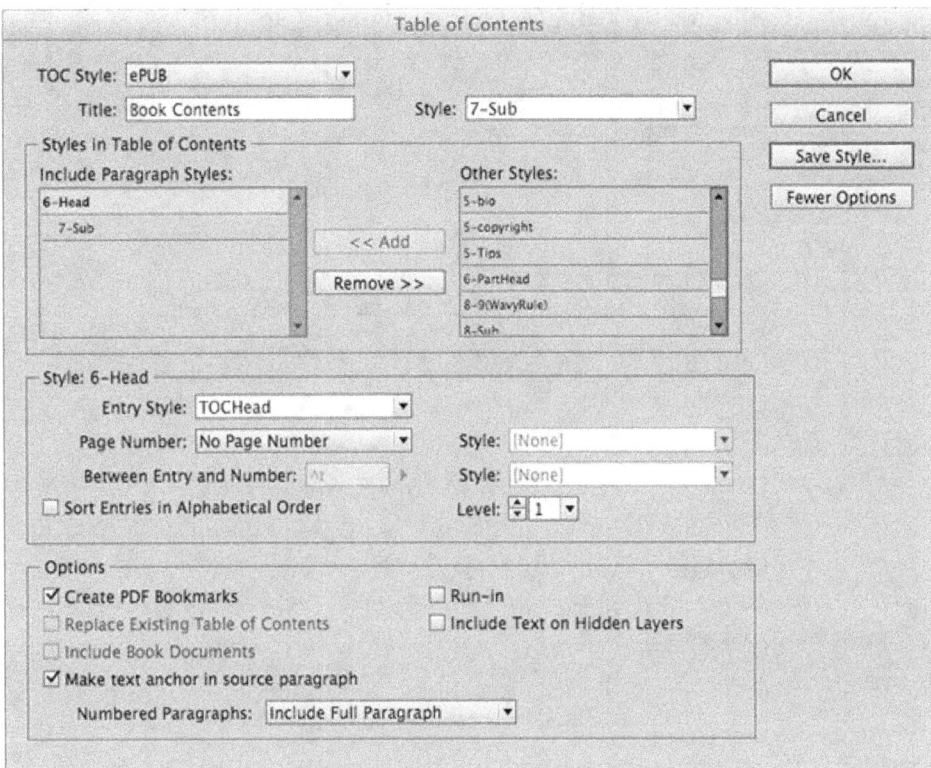

Practicality rules in these things. You can spend a lot of time and money trying to figure out why these things are so or you can publish books. Keep working on ideas. As you add a new technique that works, implement it. InDesign CC will continue to get better. But the basic concept is that you can only do what the software enables. A double-minded person will get nothing done.

I publish.

Writing the metadata (THIS IS REQUIRED)

You need to write the metadata before you export the ePUB. However, with CC 2014, you enter the metadata within the export ePUB dialog box. You can see above the old File Info dialog box. The important things here are the title, description, keywords, and copyright. You worked all this out when you released your book for print. Right? You find this dialog in the File menu under the File Info command. It is required to fill out this description page. It contains the information primarily used by the search engine spiders. So, obviously it will greatly help as your readers try to find a book like yours.

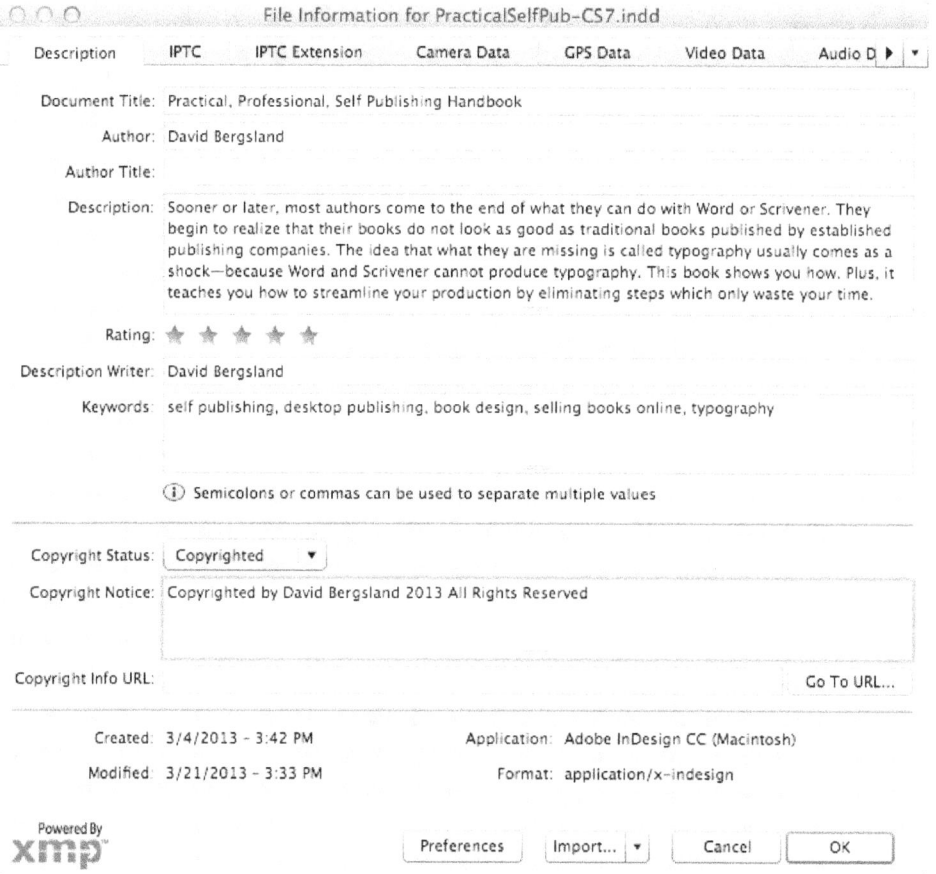

There are some strict rules for Lulu and Smashwords

Some of these rules are Apple's rules. However, many of them seem to be Lulu and Smashwords paranoia. It doesn't matter. **Do what they ask.** You do want to sell your ePUBs, right? They include things like the metadata title must be identical to the copy found on the cover. It must be in title case except for a half dozen or so tiny words. There are several others things like this. For example, I had the title of an earlier edition as: Writing In InDesign Second Edition. Lulu made me change Second Edition to a subtitle. I was very irritated, but you can't fight city hall. Here are just a few from Lulu's page (these materials are three years old now. Get the latest versions on the Lulu Website). Their list of rules is much longer: In fact, if they didn't sell so many books they would not be worth the effort.

- **Title must match everywhere:** metadata, cover, and book's title page

- **No mention of included materials that don't exist in the digital product:** (Example: CD, poster, etc.).

- **Cannot up-sell to a version of the product that is more complete.**

- **No advertisements or links.**

- **Do not use characters which require entity references in the description:** (Example: &, -, or —, curly quotes, etc.).

- **Cannot mislead buyers or misrepresent the ebook:** (Example: An illustrated guide containing no illustrations or pictures).

- **Do not use font sizes in the description**

- **Subtitles are particularly important for differentiating multiple books:** in a series that share the same title.

- **Improperly formatted HTML tags in the description:** can cause a garbled description in retail channels.

- **Titles and Subtitles incorrectly capitalized. The first letter of all words in the title and subtitle should be capitalized, except for the following words:** a, an, and, for, from, of, or, the, to. The first and last word of the title and subtitle should always be capitalized.

- **Use of HTML lists in description is forbidden**

- **Titles beginning with articles should display properly. EX:** A Tale of Two Cities, not Tale of Two Cities, A

- **Must have a valid description:** Do not use the title.

- **Multiple blank pages:** Especially at the beginning of the book. Please remember to remove blank pages before converting to ePUB.

If you do not follow all of them precisely, they will not publish your book. I just signed up with Apple Connect so I can upload my ePUBs directly. I think you can see why—I simply do not need the hassle. However, books sold through Lulu, Smashwords, and Draft2Digital continue to sell much better than the versions uploaded directly. Draft2Digital does not require much of this nonsense. They simply accept ePUB2 with no embedded fonts.

Setting the Export Tags

As mentioned, this ability to open a single dialog box and set all the HTML tags and add the CSS classes for each style is huge: It is a real disappointment that we cannot edit these class rules directly, but it makes it much easier to edit the CSS—if you're into that type of thing. CS6 was good enough for me, now CC works better, but it has added a couple of wrinkles. Nothing major though.

Forcing InDesign to write usable CSS

Sometimes I feel so stupid. The solution to the incomplete CSS in exported ePUBs for 5.5 and 6 is much more simple than I thought. Your mind just seems to turn a little corner and the solution pops up in front of you.

My beef with InDesign CS5.5's ePUBs was the need to edit the CSS. I've posted several times on my blog and published a couple free booklets about fixing the ePUB CSS (you'll need it, if you are still in CS5.5). What I wrote was accurate. It's not difficult, as long as you know HTML and CSS and can work in Dreamweaver to fix this stuff. But my frustration is that I don't think you should be forced into Dreamweaver to make an ePUB. It turns out that what I wrote simply is not necessary in most cases.

You can easily force InDesign to write good CSS

Well, that's a bit of an overstatement. The Web developer purists will be shrieking. But, you can easily make InDesign write CSS that controls all of your type in the ePUB in most cases. The problem was that InDesign did not define the basic tags: h1-6, p, ol, ul, and so on. It does in CS6, but I still use the tag.class naming procedure shown below. The only exception is lists. HTML lists are ugly and hard to control regardless—even if you coding directly into a Website, but CC has a solution for this problem also.

Lists: With CC, it turns out that setting the ePUBs conversion for lists to [Automatic} works well. However, the standard HTML lists will never work typographically. In the Export to ePUB dialog, Convert To Text works best. I change from

[Automatic] to p:bullet or p:number for the tag and class. This comes closer to retaining the indents and the special bullets. CC 2014 does retain custom bullets from dingbat fonts. But this does require embedded fonts.

		Edit All Export Tag				
Show: ⊙ EPUB and HTML ○ PDF						OK
Style	**Tag**	**Class**	**Split EPUB**	**Emit CSS**		Cancel
¶ [Basic Paragraph]	[Automatic]		☐	☑		
¶ 2–body	p	norm	☐	☑		
¶ 2–No first	p	nofirst	☐	☑		
¶ 2–run–in	p	runin	☐	☑		
¶ 3–Bulleted	p	bullet	☐	☑		
¶ 3–Description	p	nnobullet	☐	☑		
¶ 4–Body heads	h3	small	☐	☑		
¶ 5–Tips	p	tip	☐	☑		
¶ 6–Head	h1	normh1	☑	☑		
¶ 7–Sub	h2	normh2	☐	☑		
¶ 8–9(WavyRule)	h2	italic	☐	☑		
¶ 8–Sub	h3	normh3	☐	☑		
¶ TOC Heads	h1	indexhead	☐	☑		
¶ TOC Sub1	h4	indexsub	☐	☑		
A 1–bodyBOLD	strong	body		☑		
A 1–List Bold	strong	sans		☑		
A 2–Italic	em	bodyitalic		☑		
A 3–BoldItalic	span	smash		☑		
A 3–ListRegular	span	sansreg		☑		
A 4–Version	span	smallsans		☑		
A Bullet	span	red		☑		
A 14 point	span	fourteen		☑		
⊡ [Basic Graphics Frame]	[Automatic]			☑		
⊡ [Basic Text Frame]	[Automatic]			☑		
⊡ 3–Inline	[Automatic]	three		☑		
⊡ 4–Anchored	[Automatic]	four		☑		
⊡ 5–SimpleAnchor	[Automatic]	five		☑		
⊡ 6–Left	[Automatic]	six		☑		

The good news is that cracking the ePUB and editing the CSS is no longer necessary: You can easily force InDesign to write CSS rules that will control all of your type without the need to edit the CSS afterward. What you need to do is make sure that you specify a class for all your styles as well as a tag. The first thing I do is choose the Select All Unused command and delete all usused styles that were selected [except for styles which will be used for the TOC].

Let's take a look at what I just exported for an ePUB with a recent book. I opened the Edit All Export Tags...

dialog and set up the tags and classes. You can see them on the previous page. I now do the same with the Object styles.

Notice I added tags for all the styles. I do not leave any set to [Automatic]. The CC difference is this: if you do not use unique classes for every style InDesign will scream bloody murder with alerts. I tended to do it like I do with my websites, using the same class for all items in a div. But for an ePUB, this does not work. So instead of: p.norm; and h1.norm I have to use something like p.norm, and h1.normh1. It's a minor irritant and it does solve the problems. The CSS exports flawlessly.

I must decide whether the paragraph style is a subset of p, h1-h6. For character styles, I need to decide if the style is a subset of em, strong, or span. This will work, and it will look remarkably close to what I see in InDesign. I'm no longer editing the CSS in Dreamweaver. In fact, I was so sick of it I quit a little early with CS6. CC improved things. Now with CC2014 things are better, and CCNext better yet.

Now, with CC 2014, I also change the Object styles on the bottom. Instead of [Automatic] I use [div]. I try to avoid using automatic anything. Remember the best you can hope for with any automatic setting is average.

Why add the classes?

That's simple. InDesign would not define p, my basic paragraph tag. But it will define p.norm. It will not define h2, but it will define h2.normh2. Is the result wonderfully sleek and elegant XHTML code? No. But it works and all of your typography is controlled. If you do not do this, you are forced to crack the ePUB, open template.css, and add the basic tags. So, the choice is yours.

You can now design your ePUB edition of your book in InDesign and directly upload the resultant ePUB with no modifications. The results will look very good. Purists will tear their hair, but I think it's silly to add coding which does not help much—especially with ereaders being so bad.

The goal is an easily readable book—not the production of a coded tour de force. You need to closely examine the output for readability. That's your priority.

But there are always problems...

Eliminating bad fonts

The problem is that during the massive conversion from your print version to your ePUB version it is likely that you have many styles or locally formatted type that use fonts you cannot use in an ePUB. A couple of years ago, I was looking at the CSS for the first proof of the ePUBs and at the bottom I found many spans asking for fonts I was certain I was not using. They had been added along with old copy.

Below, we see the Find Font dialog box (Type>> Find Font...) for the *Writing In InDesign* book. As you can see, the top listings are many fonts I don't want to use in my ePUB, because every ereader would substitute them out into its defaults unless they were embedded [and for some I do not have an ePUB license]. I am using 130 fonts so far. Obviously this is real problem with an ereader like the Nook which only has three fonts available. More importantly, you must be

Find Font

130 Fonts in Document

Fonts in Graphics: 72
Missing Fonts: 0

Font Information	Sync
Adobe Caslon Pro Regular	
Adobe Garamond Pro Regular	
Adobe Jenson Pro Display	
Amico Regular	
Amitale Book Bold	
Amitale Book Book	
Arturo Book Regular	

Done
Find First
Change
Change All
Change/Find
More Info

Reveal in Finder   Sync Fonts

Replace With:

Font Family: Minion Pro

Font Style: Regular

☑ Redefine Style When Changing All

Font Sync is powered by Typekit.com Learn More

sure it is legal for you to use them. None of these 130 fonts are available on any ereader unless I embed the fonts.

I will use this dialog extensively to check the ePUB version of this book. I must eliminate any font for which I have no license. Plus, I do it simply to control the file size of the ePUB which is already huge, I must convert all of these fonts to graphics. I will carefully decide what to do with each one of those instances where a font is used—deciding how to convert it to a graphic you can read easily.

In addition, I must carefully examine my style usage because I still have to upload ePUBs with no fonts embedded for most of the vendors.

If I click the More Info button you can see in the Find Font dialog, it will show me the page location of the font use. Once I locate the font flagged in the actual copy of the book, *I find I have one of three issues to deal with:*

- **It may be in a paragraph or character style that was never redefined:** In that case I can redefine the style and eliminate the font usage very easily.

- **It may be in a graphic:** In this case I must make a rasterized version of the graphic. Live type in a graphic will normally cause too many problems in the display of the type to be used. Sidebars with live type are always going to be a very tricky thing in an ePUB.

- **It may be part of the copy:** This will probably not happen to you unless you are like me and write about typography and fonts. In this case, you can select the type and Create Outlines—leaving the outlines type inline in the copy. That will work, but InDesign will convert that outlined type into a coarse bitmap that looks pretty chewed up. Your best choice (for quality) is to rasterize that type in Photoshop and save it as a high quality JPEG at 72 dpi, 600 pixels wide. You can then place that high resolution bitmap graphic as an anchored object in your copy and it will look as good as possible.

 **This may add many graphics to your ebooks:** If you have books like mine which are written about book design, you have some unique problems. I had to make many new graphics to show simple things I could easily demonstrate in print like ligatures, small caps, oldstyle figures, small cap figures, ordinals, ornaments, and so on.

Once you have your fonts cleaned up and your export tags set, you should always recheck your TOC settings and your File Info. Then you can export your ePUB. Type Command+E and select ePUB for your format.

EPUB Export dialogs: fixed layout, reflowable, 2 & 3

With InDesign 5.5, the ePUB export dialog gave us a lot of tools and options as we fought to control our output. There were three pages and many things you needed to set. CS6 ramped it up even higher with the choices for ePUB 2.0.1, ePUB 3.0, and ePUB 3.0 with Layout. CC 2014 drops the 3.0 with Layout but adds fixed layout.

At this point, ePUB 2 is necessary for NookPress, Smashwords, and Draft2Digital. ePUB3 with embedded fonts works very well for iBooks and the Kindle conversion. Kobo Writing Life accepts FXL ePUBs. I am still checking its ePUB3 support for reflowable. This entire area is changing, seemingly by the week, so any updates will be mentioned in my blogs.

The Fixed Layout ePUB export dialog

This is all ePUB 3. In many ways, this option simplifies things a great deal. Fonts are always embedded, for example.

The general page

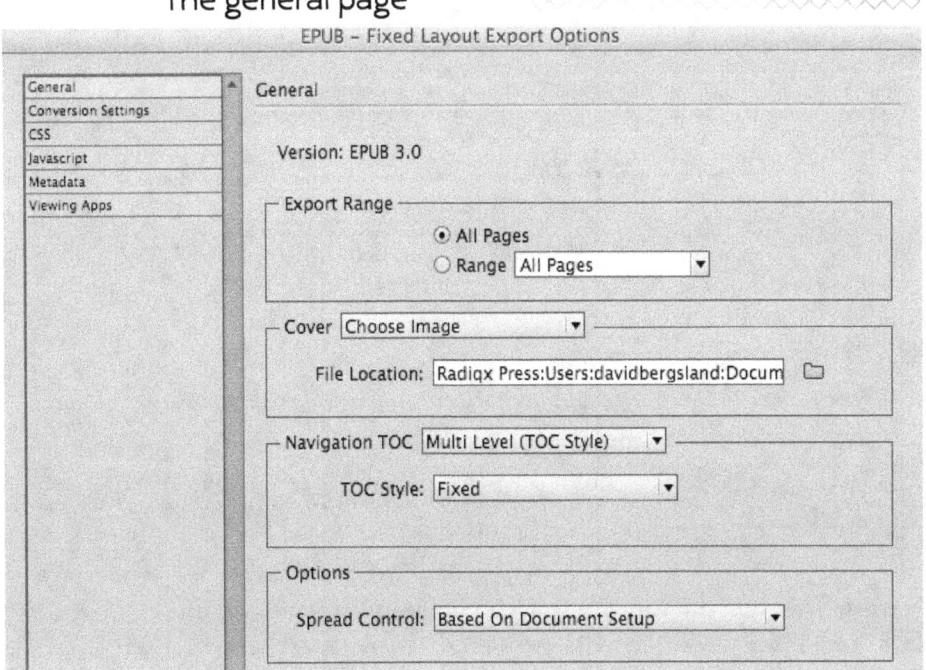

Export Range: This gives us the normal choices.
Cover: The choices are None, Rasterize First Page and Choose Image. IMHO: you always want Choose Image. Just pick one

that matches the page size. Once you choose an image that changes to From File as you see on the next page. I design a specific front cover to be used and link it here. Just remember to use a JPEG optimized with Photoshop's Save For Web dialog for the cover, at this point.

Navigation: TOC Style: You need to choose the one you have set up for your ePUBs. I call mine ePUB.

Options: Spread Control. This is very different from anything we've had before. The choices are:

- **Based on Document Setup:**

- **Convert Spread to Landscape page:** Portrait books with facing pages and converted to landscape spreads

- **Enable Synthetic spreads:** Portrait books non-facing can allow synthetic spreads if the ereader supports it.

- **Disable Spreads:** Obvious

Conversion settings

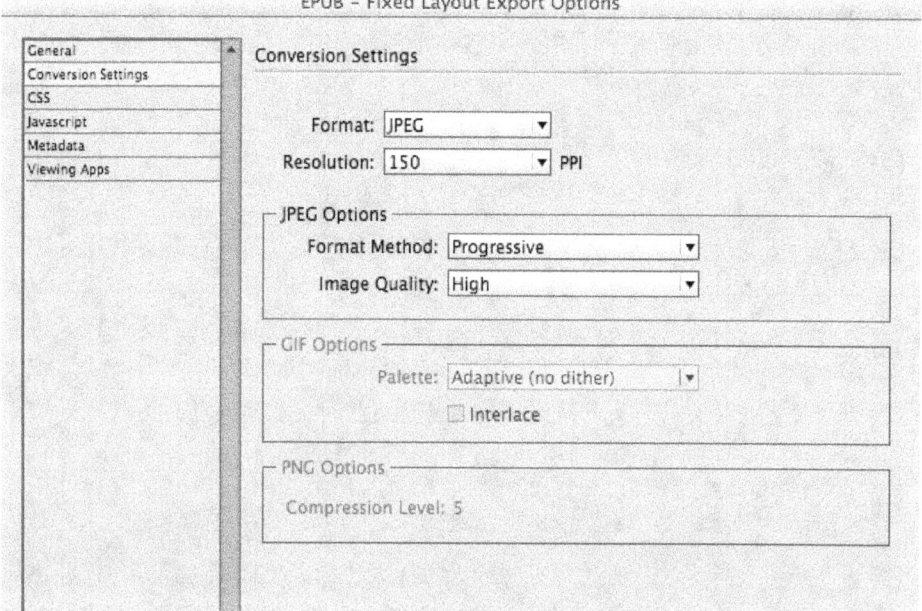

Format: This has the four basic Web choices: Automatic, JPEG, GIF, and PNG.

Resolution: Also has four choices: 72, 96, 150, or 300 dpi. I've been using 150 dpi as I have tested this out. It seems to work in fixed layout. 72 dpi seems too crude.

JPEG Options: I've been using Progressive, and High as you can see. In my current workflow, I only use JPEGs. But I can see that for transparency I'll need to go to PNGs.

GIF Options: I don't usually use these, but adaptive (no dither) is probably the best.

The real problem: I do not want InDesign to be messing up my graphics. Reconversions always blur the image, at least slightly. So, I'm doing everything I can to avoid that issue. It's not easy and often it just doesn't work. As I get clearer info from Adobe, I'll edit this and post about it in *The Skilled Workman*.

CSS & Javascript

I'm skipping over these. They simply have an attachment button to add your own CSS files or javascripts.

Metadata

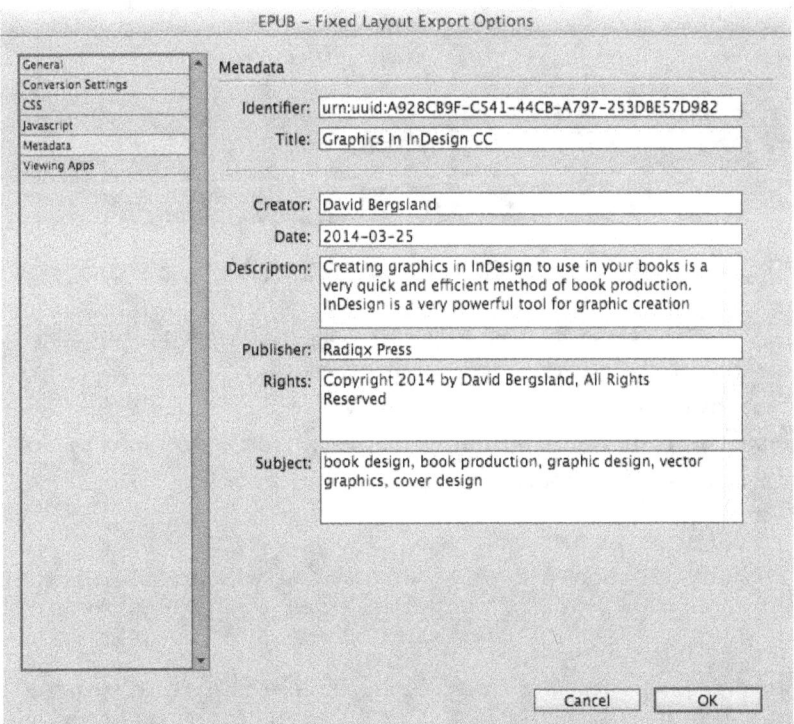

This is a major change for CC 2014. From now on we will be filling out our metadata in the Export ePUB dialog box. If you already have the File Info metadata dialog filled out—and that is certainly possible if you are making a conversion from your print PDF to a fixed layout ePUB—InDesign will populate this page from the first page of the File Info dialog. As you all should know by now, this is extremely important information. It is often the major way readers find your ePUBs.

Viewing Apps

This is the expansion of the old View ePUB after export checkbox. Now you can list the ereaders you have on your computer and view your new ePUB in all of them.

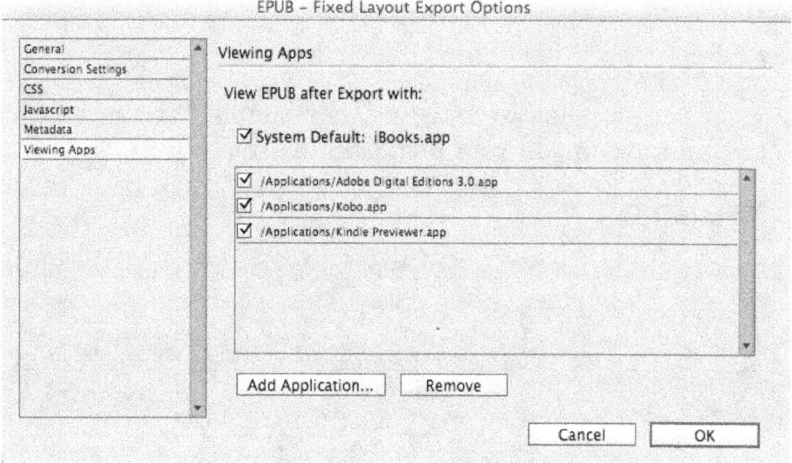

Reflowable ePUB dialog box

This covers 2.0.1 as well as 3.0 as ePUB 2 is still needed for the distributors who will not accept ePUB3 like: Lulu, Smashwords, Draft2Digital, Tomely, NookPress, and all the rest. These suppliers will not accept embedded fonts. Why do we bother with them? They sell a lot of books.

General

Version: the choices are 2.0.1 or 3.0. You will probably need several versions of this. A 3.0 fixed, a 3.0 reflow with fonts, and a 2.0.1 without fonts.

Cover: The choices are None, Rasterize First Page and Choose Image. IMHO: you always want Choose Image. Just pick one that is 600 x 800 pixels x 72 dpi. Use Photoshop's Save For Web dialog. Thats what they all want. Once you choose an image that changes to From File as you see on the next page. I design a specific front cover to be used and link it here.

EPUB – Reflowable Layout Export Options

General

General

Version: EPUB 2.0.1

Cover Choose Image

File Location: Radiqx Press:Users:davidbergsland:Docum

Navigation TOC Multi Level (TOC Style)

TOC Style: Fixed

Content

Order: Based on Page Layout

☑ Split Document

○ Single Paragraph Style 6-Head

◉ Based on Paragraph Style Export Tags

Cancel   OK

Navigation: TOC Style: You need to choose the one you have set up for your ePUBs. I call mine ePUB.

Content: Based on Page Layout, Same As XML Structure, and Same As Articles Panel. I find the articles panel useless for dealing with sidebars and the like. The only thing it works for is the TOC and Index, but those are added correctly by the page layout.

Split document: You can check the first option and pick the one paragraph style you use for starting new chapters. Or you can check Based On Paragraph Style Export Tags. In most cases, you want the second one as iBooks uses that whether or not you have the first button checked.

Text

Options

Remove Forced Line Breaks: That's what they are calling soft returns. You must remove them because the type re-wraps horribly when the readers change the size and font (and they will). When InDesign CS6 or better removes these soft returns it replaces them with a space [CS5.5 did not]. That is almost always what you want. But check and make sure.

Footnote placement: At the end of the paragraph seems to be the best method for readability of footnotes in an ereader—at least until the pop-up footnotes are accepted by everyone. There is no way to easily go to footnotes located elsewhere. Most footnotes these days are hyperlinks anyway—where you might actually hope that readers stopped the reading to go and read the source.

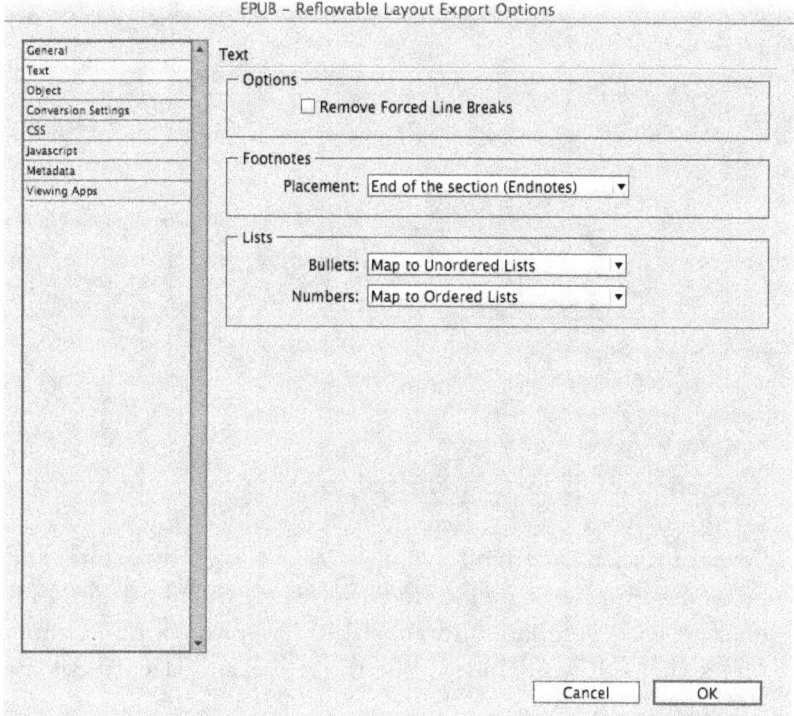

Lists
Bullets & Numbers: As mentioned, HTML lists are very ugly. With CC, the best option is Convert To Text. It's not perfect, but the bullets are maintained and any applied character style, plus this comes the closest to the indents you set up in InDesign. But remember, bullets which are dependent upon a font will need that font embedded—and we know what trouble that is at this point in ePUB distribution.

Object

This is all puzzling. But for most cases, what you see above works best. Fixed CSS Size only seems to work with iBooks. The basic concept is simple: now that it is possible to specify your original image—the one you carefully prepare in Photoshop—you are a fool to do anything else. You check Use Existing Image for Graphic Objects. You really do not want any software automatically doing anything to your images when they are so severely limited by the format. Web images, 72 dpi, are extremely crude. Virtually all detail is lost

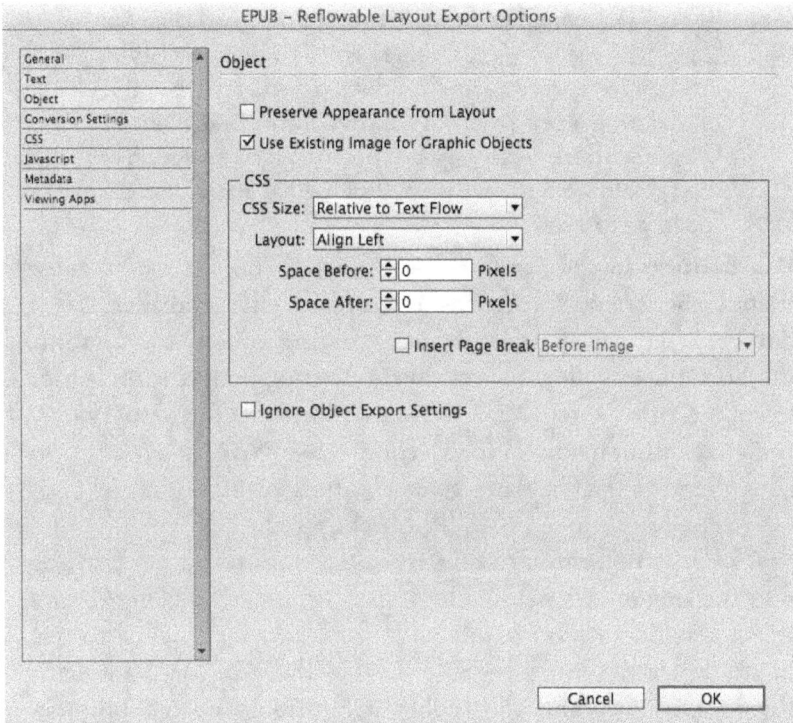

Finding out information on images is like trying to pull hens' teeth (and no, city folk, they don't have teeth). No one seems to want to admit how bad the images really are. The best I can find is that the iPad, most smart phones, and high-resolution tablets require 600x800 pixels or less.

- The iPad maximum is 600x860 pixels.
- Nook's maximum size is 600x730 pixels.
- For Kobo and Fire it is 600x800.

At this point, I make my images to size, and JPEG [in almost all cases]. I make them wide enough to fit the column of type and place them as Anchored Objects. With CC2014, I can use smaller images more easily. But tall narrow images will always be a problem. I try to do something to make the images wider so I can use the Above Line style if the image is tall. I do this to get as much help as I can with image sharpness. You can make them smaller and have them work OK. But, if you need detail make them as large as possible, and that is 600 wide portrait, and 800 wide landscape.

Remember, ebook graphics are ghastly: I continue to fight the good fight, but you really need to question why you are even including graphics. The iPad does a good job, but the ePUB format itself does not support graphic excellence. Of course there was the hope that the high resolution of the tablets would really help. But the file size is usually too large to use.

Use Existing Image for Graphic Objects: The InDesign auto-mated conversion processes re-rasterize the graphics. So, I am very pleased with the Use Existing Image for Graphic Objects button. My procedure is to open all the graphics from the print version in Photoshop and make them exactly the pixel dimension I need. Then I use Save For Web… to save them as JPEGs. This gives the best results.

For print, I use PSDs (Photoshop's native format) at 300 dpi. I keep the original PSDs in case I want to go back to the way the image was before the JPEG compression. Then I save JPEG versions at 600 pixels wide [or whatever I need] to use in the ePUB. I should be able double the size for iPads with Retina Displays (and the higher resolution Android tablets), but it adds so much to the file size I haven't bothered yet.

Preserve Appearance from Layout: This is now unchecked when I check Use Original Image. The appearance is con-trolled by the Objects styles.

CSS size: The choices are Fixed and Relative to Page. I use Relative to Page, but again this is controlled by the controls in the object style. I want them as large as possible to be readable because they are basically low-res bitmap images. Fixed works well with iBooks but not elsewhere.

Image Alignment and Spacing: Because my images are all anchored objects, the alignment is controlled by the object style used. But I set Flush left.

Insert page break: Before Image, After Image, or Both Before and After Image. I've never used it, but I can see its utility.

Ignore Object Export Settings: I leave it unchecked because I do not set custom settings for any image. The problem was that Object Export Settings were needed to control anchored objects as sidebars. In CS6 and earlier, these settings really didn't work. Now they are not necessary.

Conversion

Format: You have four options: Automatic, JPEG, GIF, and PNG. I use JPEGs almost exclusively. With Automatic on, InDesign converts anything it can't use [like a PDF] to a PNG. The uses of GIFs are negligible in my workflow.

Resolution (ppi): I make my large images 600 pixels wide and 72 dpi JPEGs. I've been using 150 dpi for fixed layout books with fewer graphics. For a book like *Writing In InDesign* with over 260 graphics, I go with 72 dpi to better handle the size of the resulting ePUB.

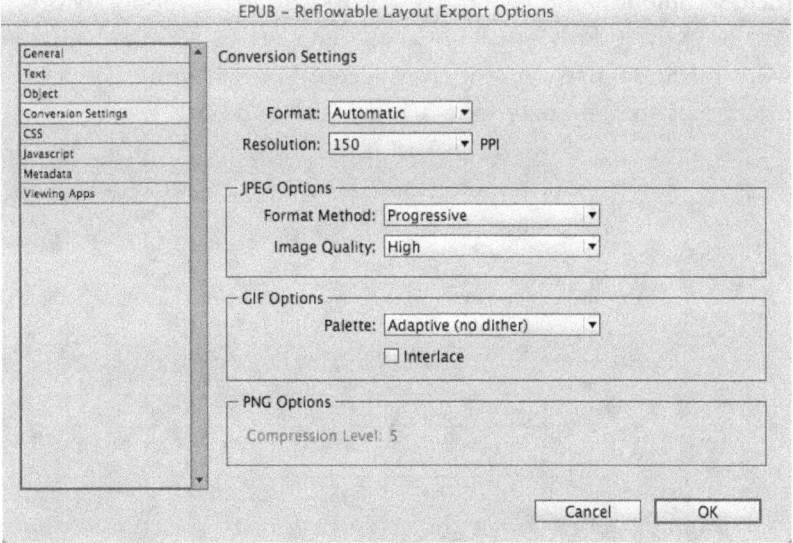

JPEG Options: I set the JPEG options to Progressive, High. The image quality in ePUBs is bad enough without JPEG artifacts produced by compressing the JPEGs too far. For my font design book (with nearly 300 graphics) this made my ePUB nearly 20 MB. But then the ePUB for the professional InDesign book is 22.3 MB. The one for this book will be less than 10 MB. So, I am sometimes forced to change the quality to medium. Because the images are almost all screen captures, the new ePUB looks very good on the iPad. I may have to do that for this book also. You must do what you need to do to get the best images possible.

GIF Options: I use Adaptive (no dither). But then, if I make my GIFs with Photoshop's Save for Web, I'll use 100% dither and a bit of lossy compression.

PNG Options: I take what I get.

CSS

Generate CSS: Unlike fixed layout, where CSS is not optional, it is in reflowable. I can't really think of a reason why you would not want to generate CSS—except for the obvious one: your own CSS is better and you want to use it.

Page Margins: Try it, but most ereaders ignore these.

Preserve Local Overrides: I uncheck this. You usually do not want any local overrides. They are all covered with your character styles.

Include embeddable Fonts: This works for the iBooks Store and for Kindle Previewer when you convert to Kindle. It may work for Kobo also. I know they accept Fixed Layout which is ePUB 3.0, so they may take a reflowable 3.0 with fonts.

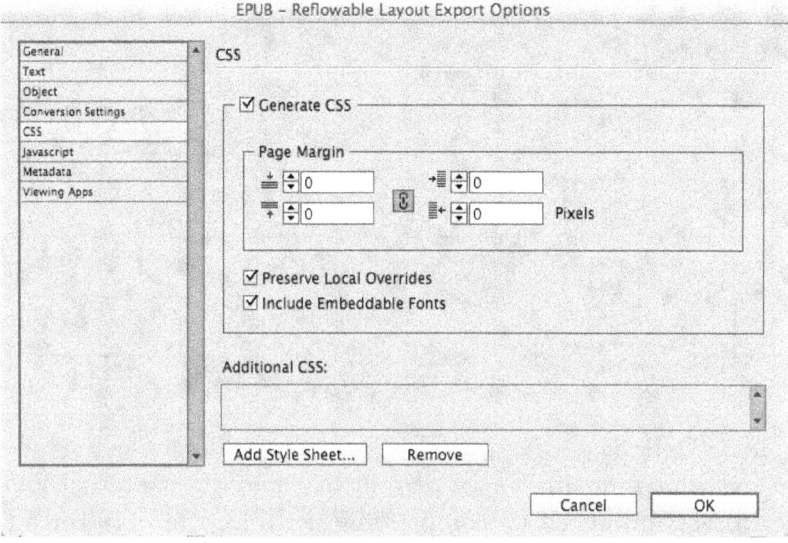

Javascript

I'm skipping over this. It simply has an attachment button to add your own javascripts.

Metadata

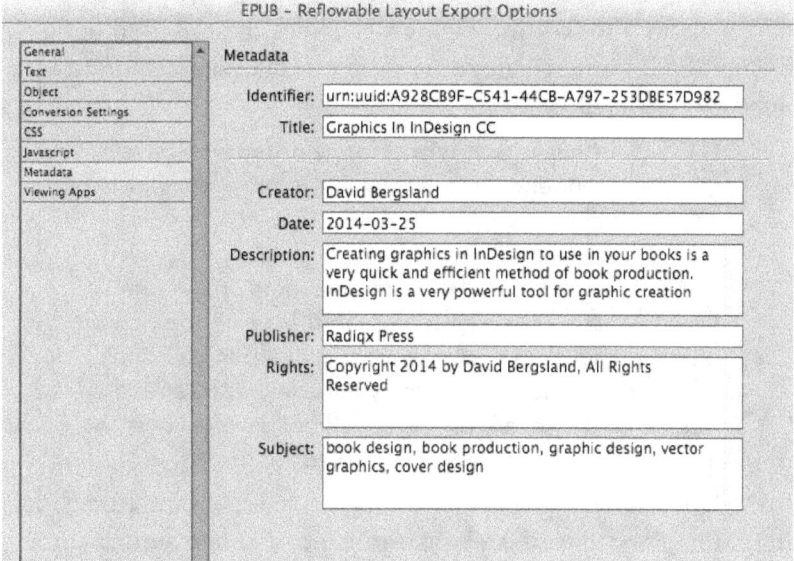

This is a major change for CC 2014. From now on we will be filling out our metadata in the Export ePUB dialog box. If you already have the File Info metadata dialog filled out—and that is certainly possible if you are making a conversion from your print PDF to a fixed layout ePUB—InDesign will populate this page from the first page of the File Info dialog. As you all should know by now, this is extremely important information. It is often the major way readers find your ePUBs.

Viewing Apps

View after Exporting: Always check this. This has changed for me lately now that the third version of Adobe Digital Editions is out. But ADE3 is still quite bad. Readium [requires Chrome] is fairly good. Now that iBooks is in OSX Mavericks, that is the best option. Always look over the exported ePUB in ADE3 before you validate and upload. You also need to check in iBooks. Increasingly, I check it out in BlueFire on my iPad. I am still regularly surprised by something that needs to be fixed.

 Always test with crappy ereaders: I have a tendency to only test in the ereaders which show everything. Quite regularly I am surprised and disgusted with what is actually displayed in Nook, Kobo, or the e-ink ereaders in general. Basically, that means you need to test using the apps on your iPad. You don't have an iPad? Then you don't really have to worry because you have crappy already well-defined by everything except Readium and Fire.

This is not a smooth process yet. It is really good that InDesign can now export ePUBs that can be validated. But it is not smooth yet—and probably not be uneventful until InDesign 11 or so. InDesign CC2014 is getting pretty good, but there is still a long ways to go.

Click OK and you've got an ePUB

It will open in your reader of choice. Proof it carefully in a variety of ereading apps or hardware. Redo as necessary. You will quickly develop a good idea of what is translating well and what does not work for you. I need to reiterate: proof carefully and often. You need to go through every ePUB you export page by page. Adobe Digital Editions 3 is a real problem. It can not use many of the new capabilities, plus it will show fonts from your hard drive on your computer which will not show in your ereader. On the other hand, do not be seduced by iBooks. It's in another league. Most ereaders will not do nearly as well as you see in iBooks.

Validate it

Redo the proof as often as necessary. When you have what you like, go to: http://validator.idpf.org/ for validation. It should validate. If it does not, all I can do is pray you will be given information that will enable you to figure it out. The failure messages tend to be very cryptic. But Lulu, Smashwords, and validator.idpf.org are getting much better about this and increasingly they let you know what is causing the problem in a manner you can understand (this was not true two years ago). Lulu now lets you know the specific problem and Smashwords gives pretty good hints. If your ePUB is over 10 MB [the online limit], get your own ePUB Checker.

One problem with the CC ePUBs

One of the major changes in CC is the rewriting of the export engine to re-arraign and rename some of the files within the ePUB archive [it's just a renamed ZIP archive, as you recall]. This makes embedded fonts work with iBooks. However, red flags fly over at Lulu, Draft2Digital, and Smashwords because they were used to it the other way. The ePUBs validate but ePUB distributors will not accept them.

So, if that happens, IDML your CC files back to CS6 and export the ePUB there: These older style ePUBs work fine with Lulu and Smashwords.

Uploading to the various places

Before you even think of doing this make sure that you have the following under control.

- The book's title
- The book's subtitle (Optional)
- The description
- The price
- The keywords

Without all of these things well in hand, the uploading process to the various suppliers will much more complicated than you want it to be. Plus, you will have a hard time being consistent. If you are not consistent, your book will be listed in various ways in various places. Your readers will be confused. Google will be confused. Amazon will be confused. You do not want that.

You will also need to make a special rasterization of your cover for each vendor. They all have different size requirements. This is one of the main reasons I suggest you have your front cover separate in PDF form. That way each rasterization will be sharp and crisp. At this point, most will accept the Kindle requirement which is 1563 x 2500 pixels at 72 dpi. But make sure.

Never forget these are Web documents

Actually, as you know, they are not exactly that. There are many Web page possibilities which cannot be used in an ePUB. But, the basic capabilities are the same. You are using HTML and CSS with 72 dpi images a maximum of 600 pixels wide in almost all cases.

CHAPTER EIGHT

Converting to Kindle

Until the summer of 2012, I gave some very explicit instructions for the hand construction of the HTML and CSS needed to step back in time to Amazon's MOBI format. It was extremely limited in what was allowed. It was all done by writing HTML by hand. Things have gotten a lot better. In fact, in many ways, Kindle's KF8 Export Plug-in for CS6 and earlier worked very well. You could export a Kindle book easily, though it was missing many capabilities.

Now with CC things have changed again. There was a short time period where Amazon's plug-in was doing better than converting an ePUB. This was also the same time frame where Amazon was bouncing all MOBIs made with non-Amazonian software. But now you can just upload your ePUB from InDesign and it converts well.

Kindle Previewer

One of the less heralded features of Amazon's free Kindle Previewer is that is will do a good job of converting an ePUB using Kindle Gen—my current production workflow.

- **First I export an ePUB with embedded fonts:** for the iBooks Store.

- **Next I package the document used to create the ePUB into a new folder:** in the Amazon folder for the Kindle version.

- **In the newly packaged Links folder, I go through all the linked graphics:** [They are all JPEGs at 100% quality to avoid artifacts].

- **Any graphic which is over 125 KB:** I use Edit Original to open it into Photoshop.

- **I use Save For Web to get the file size of the graphics adjusted to less than 125 KB:** A couple of times I have saved them at exactly 127 KB and Amazon still resized them—thereby ruining them.

- **If I do that, I Save As a PSD:** and save the original JPEG as a PSD in a new Originals folder.

- **Change all the object styles to your Above Line option, flush left or centered:** Often the fancy anchored objects options are stripped out by Kindle.

- **When all the graphics are fixed, I export a new ePUB:** I open it in Kindle Previewer to convert it to a KF8 package for KDP uploads. I use that to proof, but lately I've just been uploading the ePUB in KDP.

So far, the results have been good. I am sticking with this new procedure at least until Amazon's new plug-in comes out [if it does]. Who knows what they will do to ramp up their offering? If I change back I'll blog about it.

The CS6 Kindle Export plug-in

At this point, there is no CC plug-in. This is fairly important. I have heard several stories about Kindle book producers who had their book bounced by Amazon because it was not produced with Amazon's tools. There are three of them with a free download from Amazon: the InDesign Kindle Export plug-in, KindleGen, and Kindle Previewer.

- **For CC, the plug-in is gone.**

- **KindleGen is a command-line app:** (meaning everything is done in raw code).

- **Kindle Previewer is what we use to see what the Kindle book looks like after we export the ePUB:** It uses KindleGen to convert the new CC ePUBs to KF8 books and then views them. However, if you use Fixed for the CSS Size the preview graphic sizes will be very small. I am told that this is not an issue once the book is viewed in your Kindle. But I don't have one.

Images

Basically, nothing is changed here. For CS6 and earlier, I still recommend that you place all images inline. For CC ePUBs, all images are changed into anchored objects. Kindle Previewer seems to strip out a lot of that information. Quality issues with the Kindle books still remain very frustrating. I imagine it is much easier to deal with if you have a Fire.

The Kindle supports GIF, BMP, JPEG, PNG images in your content. Vector graphics are not supported and must be converted to raster graphics. **The size limit for images is 127KB.** Below this limit, all images will be exported unaltered. While above this limit, images will be automatically optimized [re-rasterized] to be under the size limit during conversion. You should understand this to mean that images larger than 125KB will be ruined. That is straight forward enough.

Here's another warning from Amazon about images with text:

I'll just quote them on this:

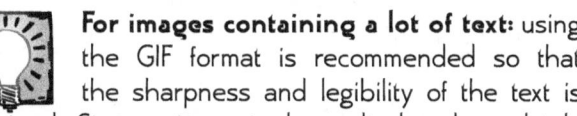

For images containing a lot of text: using the GIF format is recommended so that the sharpness and legibility of the text is retained. Since an image is always displayed completely on the screen, image resolution should be constrained to a maximum of 500x600 [ed: 600w x 500h] so that the image is not scaled, making it hard to read. Minimum font size should be such that a lower-case "a" is at least 6 pixels tall. You can reduce the number of colors used in an image to optimize its size or split the image horizontally to keep it under the size limit. It is highly recommended that automatic optimization by KindleGen be avoided in case of images containing text.

My recommendation is that you do what you need to do to entirely avoid any "optimization" by making your images smaller than 125K and 600 pixels wide or narrower. Notice they specify that images larger than 600x500 pixels will be scaled. This means that you need to keep the height less than 500 pixels also.

Cover image

It's required and it needs to be exactly 600x800. In the past JPEGs were virtually required. I found that unless they were produced by Photoshop's Save for Web command I had troubles. I set up my images exactly to spec before placing them into my InDesign document.

The KDP upload process will have you upload the cover image again in addition to the one embedded in your book, for their use. Their exact recommendation is 1563 pixels by 2500 pixels. It's all pretty straight forward. The KDP Publishing guidelines are linked off the plug-in page. My basic design recommendations remain the same as we discussed for ePUBs, modified only by what you see above.

Bottomline on the Kindle Export Plug-In & Previewer

Since the summer of 2012, everything I've exported with the new plug-in worked as expected and has been accepted by KDP. Then I used Kindle Previewer—which also worked well. Now I upload the CC ePUBs directly in KDP. If I come up with a new and better procedure, I'll keep you up to date on *The Skilled Workman*. The big thing to remember is that the fancy features only work in the Fire, several only in Fire HD and HDX.

Dealing with the old e-ink
Kindles, Nooks, & Kobos

These remain popular and for graphic designers, this is horrible news. All anchored object stying is stripped out and the images are placed on their own line flush left. All font information is stripped out—including the serif and sans serif distinctions. I would be concerned about much more.

I imagine tables are dumped. The only borders kept are those rasterized within the Photoshop images. These e-ink ereaders are very much like reading your book in NotePad or TextEdit. But, novels are very simple books.

PERSONAL NOTE

Colophon:

This book has been written in my small office at the back of our 132 year old [1881], two-story framed home in southern Minnesota—Mankato to be specific: It is a beautiful old section of this small city with streets lined with large, mature trees, brick and framed two and three story homes, near the bottom of the large (200-300 foot) bluffs lining the Minnesota River valley in this area. This is part of the view through the window next to my built-in desk. Actually it was the view last August 2013.

I have a 21.5" late 2013 iMac running Mavericks with 16gb ram, an old Epson scanner, and cable modem access to the Web. I'm using Adobe's InDesign CC 2014 for this book along with the latest update for Photoshop CC.

For the fonts, I designed the basic fonts used in this book in FontLab 5—though my most recent fonts have been designed for my new book on font design using Fontographer 5.1. The fonts were designed as part of my personal best seller, *Practical Font Design 3rd Edition Plus*. The serif faces are from the eight font Contenu family and the headers are from the companion font family I designed for Contenu: Buddy. For ePUBs like this, I have a Contenu Ebook family I designed.

I produced all the graphics as well, though there are several royalty-free photos scattered in the book. The captures were mainly done with Snapz Pro X, though I used GrabIt for timed captures.

As usual, it has been great fun putting this book together for you. I pray it's helpful for you in your work.

Today, it's a cool and dry day in July. It almost feels like Fall. Gorgeous weather. I'm going out to work in the garden for a while.

Friday, July 18, 2014 • Mankato, Minnesota

SOCIAL MEDIA

My online addresses:

My technical blog: http://bergsland.org
My Christian blog: http://radiqx.com
My normal email: david@radiqx.com

FaceBook: https://www.facebook.com/radiqxpress
Pinterest: http://www.pinterest.com/radiqxpress/
Gumroad: https://gumroad.com/radiqxpress
Twitter [Christian]: @radiqxpress
Twitter [technical]: @davidbergsland
Google+: +DavidBergsland
Scribd: http://www.scribd.com/bergsland

Book availability

Search for David Bergsland for the books listed on the bookstore site you prefer. Almost all of my books are on Amazon [Kindle & print], Nook, the iBooks Store, Kobo, Smashwords, Scribd, and many other locations where the various distributors having gotten the books listed.

I have an author page on Amazon.

Thank you for reading my book,

Index

www.ingramcontent.com/pod-product-compliance
Lightning Source LLC
Chambersburg PA
CBHW080230200526
45165CB00026B/3380